The Invisible Foes
She Encounters

*To my special Friend Vicki
From Sandy Beauchamp*

The Invisible Foes
She Encounters

SL Beauchamp

Copyright © 2008 by SL Beauchamp.

ISBN: Softcover   978-1-4257-8210-8

All rights reserved. No part of this book may be reproduced or transmitted in any form or by any means, electronic or mechanical, including photocopying, recording, or by any information storage and retrieval system, without permission in writing from the copyright owner.

True story written by SL Beauchamp.

This book was printed in the United States of America.

To order additional copies of this book, contact:
Xlibris Corporation
1-888-795-4274
www.Xlibris.com
Orders@Xlibris.com

Contents

Chapter One	The Roaring Twenties	9
Chapter Two	As A Teenager	20
Chapter Three	Sheila's Wedding	31
Chapter Four	Blossom's Diary	34
Chapter Five	The Summer Months	45
Chapter Six	Blossom's First Hope Chest	51
Chapter Seven	Blossom's Engagement	63
Chapter Eight	The Year She Concord the Invisible Foe	78
Chapter Nine	Getting a Helping Hand	89
Chapter Ten	Owning Their First Home	94
Chapter Eleven	Their Trip to Hawaii	100
Chapter Twelve	The Home Coming	114
Chapter Thirteen	Hard Times	128
Chapter Fourteen	Their Big Move	142

THIS BOOK I WOULD LIKE TO DEDICATE TO MY MOTHER AND FATHER, WHO HAVE DONE SO, MUCH FOR ME

Chapter One

The Roaring Twenties

This story of events happening throughout this entire book is based on the Author's life and knowledge. Only the names of the people and places have been changed to protect the innocent.

The story begins about a young enchanting girl growing up in a small town who had petit-mal and the invisible foes she encounters. It all began in the roaring twenties with a young couple called Abel and Ada Cartwright, living in Regina, Ada was expecting her second child at this point. Ada's first being a beautiful baby girl who we will call Cara, Cara was two when Casey was born. At the same time that Casey was born, quite a number of miles away Humphrey and Hannah, another couple were expecting their second child also. Bert their eldest son was very excited about the new baby arriving into their family.

It wasn't until seven months later after Casey was born, that Hannah had Dawn. A very frail little baby girl the most enchanting baby you ever seen. Some years later in the hungry thirties, it was then that Dawn had met Casey for the very first time. They fell in love and courted for a few short years.

Later a wedding took place in a small church on the west coast, with only a best man and a maid of honor to be present. The following day by means of telephone; they shocked their parents with the good news of their marriage. In return Casey's parents told Cara and Ralph. Cara all ready married to Jed, Cara was quite happy for her younger brother, Ralph only two years younger than Casey was also happy for them both.

Dawn had very much been welcomed into the Cartwright family. In return Dawn's Sister and Brothers, Bert, Kay, Flora, Fenton and Joy, also gave them both best wishes and warm welcome to Casey being now apart of their big family.

It wasn't too long after they were married that Casey was sent off to war to fight for his country and Dawn was left at their west coast home expecting their first child. Oh! It was hard for Dawn but she was a very strong willed woman now, she made a good home for Casey and little Sheila, Sheila was born in the midst of winter, she was only seven pounds eleven ounces at birth.

Dawn would sew little baby clothes for her in order for them to save any money. She would buy inexpensive flannel to make the diapers for baby Sheila, then the clothes that Dawn herself would have out grown she would make over into baby clothes.

For Dawn the lonely nights especially were the hardest, with Casey away fighting the war, but she managed through it ok. Casey and Dawn would write back and forth while they were apart, as time went on Casey would send little trinkets home to his darling wife from different places he had fought in. In return Dawn would bake fruit cakes and send them off to Casey at Christmas time where ever he was stationed at the time. It must of been the over whelming love and trust they had for each other that gave them the strength to keep going on.

This went on until the war had ended. Then after four years from the time that little Sheila was born, Casey's Sister Cara past away. It was a very sad time for all of them, since Casey and Dawn had been very close to Cara and her husband Jed, but in the year to follow Dawn gave birth to another baby girl weighing seven pounds four ounces.

She was born in the fall just as the leaves were about to change color, This baby girl was the most breathtaking little baby girl you ever laid your eyes on "said Dawn" big blue eyes, dark black curly hair and little stubby pink nose.

Her skin was so soft and white, just like the blossoms on an apple tree in the early spring. She reminded them so much of the white blossoms from the tree they use to sit under while courting.

Little Blossom was always into mischief that would get her into trouble. She was a very colic baby and most of the time Dawn would have to have her in one arm while trying to make dinner with the other.

When her younger sister Cynthia was born two years later, one evening around dinner time, Blossom decided that her baby sister had to have dinner too, Cynthia had just been home from the hospital not too long ; was laid upon the master bed to sleep. Blossom marched right into the bedroom where Cynthia lay asleep on their down filled quilt, spread across the double bed, she proceeded carrying her out like a sack of potatoes across her little shoulders. "I brought baby for dinner Mummy," Blossom would say to her parents as big as bold as can be, but she didn't understand why, when Dawn took Cynthia away and said No! Baby Cynthia can't come and sit at our dinner table.

Blossom would insist on going back to the bedroom for her sister and bringing her out again as if she was a dolly, until Dawn finally sat Blossom down and explained why babies don't come to a dinner table when they are as small as Cynthia. 6:11 P.M. was another incident where Cynthia was maybe a year old and Dawn had looked everywhere for Blossom, she just couldn't find her anywhere; Dawn was beginning to get worried when! All of a sudden she had heard something out in the garage which was attached to the house by a breezeway

Dawn had then decided to go out and have a look what the noise was all about, and sure enough it was Blossom, she had wondered out to the garage, was into Casey's two inch nails. Blossom had managed to spread the entire box full of nails all over the cement floor, since she hadn't seen her mother standing in the door way watching her, Dawn figured, well! at least I know where she is and she isn't really hurting anything, so with that thought in mind she left Blossom sitting playing on the cement floor in her little print dress made of cotton. Dawn had gone back into their older style house to look in on Cynthia, sleeping soundly, then to tidy up some more before Casey would be home for dinner. When Casey had finally arrived home that evening after a hard day of building homes, he was very much upset with his Blossom, for scattering those nails all over the garage floor.

Well! Casey just picked them all up with Blossom's help, a nail at a time she would bring them over to her daddy. Blossom loved her daddy very much, then Casey would put them all back into their perspective places and put the boxes high on a shelf out of Blossom's reach for the next time she would try it. When that was all finished and done with, he picked up his little girl in one arm and his lunch kit in the other, then walked into the house through the kitchen which was next to the garage door, gave Dawn a quick kiss on the cheek and went to get changed, Dawn was busy getting dinner started then.

Then a couple of months later Blossom had a bobby pin that she had managed to find laying around on the kitchen floor, in which she had proceeded to crawl over to a electrical outlet and stick the pin right into the hole of the plug in the wall socket, it was close to the floor in the kitchen near a doorway, the shock from the current had sent her flying straight across the kitchen floor. After that had happened she never did it again, she was scared of electrical outlets for a long time to come.

By now Sheila would be maybe eight and in grade two, while Cynthia would only be a year old. Cynthia was her mother's pride and joy from day one, they say she looked a lot like Dawn at birth. As time went by and Blossom would be around four now, it was then that Dawn and Casey found out that she had epilepsy, only with Blossom it was called petit-mal, a milder case of epilepsy which her parents were to find this out in the short time to come.

It all happened in their fourth home they had lived in; when Dawn noticed that there was something very wrong with her Blossom. Blossom had been ripping apart one of Dawn's very best doilies, when Dawn told Blossom to stop it, in a scolding voice, but Blossom hadn't answered her right away.

The doily was on the coffee table in front of the large picture window in the living-room, Blossom's back was to her mother. At first Dawn just thought that Blossom was being stubborn, but in a few short minutes Dawn was to realize that something was really wrong with their little girl.

Now! By the time Blossom had come out of the seizure, which only lasted a few short minutes at a time, she was very much frightened of her mother. Blossom could not understand why she had been yelling at her and chasing her down the basement stairs. You see when you have a seizure like Blossom did everything is pitch black and you don't hear anything, but you keep doing what you had started out to do, only what you say or do doesn't make any sense to anyone else.

While sitting on the bottom step trying to figure out what she had done that was so wrong to make her mother that angry with her," You see every thing Blossom had ever tried to do she did to try to make her mother proud of her, only it never worked out the way she had planned them to be. After what seemed like a long time to her thinking about what had just happened, she still couldn't figure out what the reason was for her mother to be so angry with her.

Blossom had then decided to go back upstairs, still afraid of Dawn, but very calm asked her mother what she had done that was so bad that she had to be scolded. Dawn still not believing Blossom, hadn't really known what she had done with her best doily, had continued to scold her some more.

This all happened about three o'clock in the afternoon while Casey was still at work, but by five o'clock that evening Dawn had realized that Blossom was telling the truth about her not knowing what she had done to her mother's doily.

It was from that day on that Blossom started to see doctors and having to have test after test to be taken on her brain. The doctors then had decided to put Blossom on some large white pills about four a day and later on it was increased to six a day. At first Blossom did not understand on what was going on with her, Blossom said, "that she was taken into a large medical building that had been painted mostly white, she also recalls, Blossom thinks it was some kind of a laboratory in the part of the building that she was taken into."

In that part of the building there was also another room that contained only one double bed with a pillow and a white top and bottom sheet to lie on, the top sheet had been folded neatly upon the foot of the bed.

There also was another machine in the wall at the head of the bed with a bunch of needles coming out of the middle of it, but before the nurse would take Blossom into that room to lie down, she would be seated on a wooden stool that was fairly high up from the ground for Blossom.

Just after Blossom had been seated upon that wooden stool, the nurse would proceed to mark the top of her head with a red marking pencil that was hard to wash off, which Dawn found out later just how hard it was to wash off. After about fifteen minutes marking the top of Blossom's head, she was escorted into the room with that machine in the wall and that double bed. Blossom can still recall how cold she use to get lying on that double bed with only a thin sheet to cover her little body.

As Blossom was looking out the large picture window to the left of the bed, she could see her mother looking back in watching her. Then after the nurse had stuck those needles into her head where the red markings were made, sometimes they were just taped on with special tape. The nurse all dressed in white would go out and stand on the side of the large picture window; and would be reading something that was coming out of another machine, sometimes Dawn would be standing next to the nurse.

It was always Dawn that would bring Blossom to the medical center for her treatments. Casey usually stayed home with the other children or otherwise was working. At first in that bed with just a thin sheet to keep her warm, Blossom would be very cold and scared. Sometimes Dawn would come in with her until she wasn't scared or had fallen asleep, but as Blossom would come to the medical center more often, she had grown use to it. Sometimes she fell into a deep sleep waiting for the nurse to come into the room to take those needles out from the top of her head.

Then about one or two hours later a nurse and Dawn would come back into the room and take the needles out. At that point in time Blossom didn't know what they called the machine, and then when she was all finished for the treatment, Dawn would take her out and buy her something special for being such a good girl.

In years to come Blossom was to know that, that machine in the wall was called an electrocardiograph; and that it had sent messages from her brain to the machine on the other side of that picture window. With that electrocardiograph machine with that, the message had been sent. An electroencephalogram machine is that amplifies electrical activity of various parts of the brain as peaks and valleys on a strip of paper that came out of the machine, sometimes the nurse would show Blossom the readings on it. So Blossom would go through that about once a year when she was younger, as she grew older and was starting to understand better, she didn't have to go through it as much.

Blossom would still have to take those pills as large and as white as they were. Those pills were some kind of a tranquilizer, "said Blossom. At one point she was taking up to eight pills a day. That was when she was about eight years old and her baby sister was now on the way, the doctors had to take Blossom back down to six tranquilizers a day, since she was always falling asleep in school and at home. Eights months to the day later a baby girl was born to Dawn and Casey, they named her Willette, she was only seven pounds, but very pretty. By that time Blossom was in grade two, Cynthia in grade one and Sheila in grade five. Sheila was so ashamed of her mother for having another baby at her age of thirty-six. She had thought that Dawn was too old for that sort of stuff at her age, but in weeks to come Sheila learned to love little Willette just like the rest of the family, she use to sneak peaks at her baby sister when she had thought no one else was watching, "said Dawn." Blossom had lived a very normal life even though she had that awful petit-mal hanging over her; she was determined to make the best of it.

Every birthday Blossom had, she uses to wish that the petit-mal would go away someday. Blossom thought that her petit-mal had caused a lot of problems and worries in the family and she didn't like that at all. She was always a happy go lucky type of a child with lots of energy to burn.

Sometimes the doctors would have to change her medication to another type, one that was stronger, but Dawn always made sure that she had taken her medication on time. In school Dawn would break open the capsules and mix it right into her milk in her thermos. In that way she was always sure to have gotten the right amount of medication each day.

Blossom mentioned, "She still was aloud to go to a public school with her sisters, but her parents never told any of the teachers at the school about her petit-mal, until junior high school, you see the doctors had advised them not to. There were very few of their friends that knew about Blossom's condition

Blossom would think that maybe her parents were ashamed of her because of that illness; sometimes she would wish that she was dead, because of her illness that was giving her parents so much trouble, which Blossom had thought was nothing but a lot of misery that she had brought to her family she loved so much.

Sheila, Cynthia and Blossom usually walked together on the way to school, there was only one busy highway that they had to cross on the way, then there was a sidewalk raised; that was about six inches up higher from the highway all the way through to the school yard.

The school was called Cartwright Elementary school and the children as children will be use to tease them about the name of the school being the same last name as theirs, those children use to say that the Cartwright school was named after them, but it wasn't. There was a smaller school on the grounds set back further from the Cartwright s School, that other children attended, it was for children who were mentally handicapped, one day Blossom's remembers" there was this one little boy who came over to her on the play grounds to ask her to play ball with him, but At that time Blossom couldn't understand him, then the teacher came over to bring him back to his side of the school grounds, since he wasn't suppose to be over by the elementary school grounds in the first place.

When going to grade school sometimes Dawn would drive the children on a rainy day, but that wasn't very often, "said Blossom. Not that it didn't rain that much, it seemed, that it was raining all the time. At least it did to Blossom.

Dawn just thought that it would be good exercise for them to walk, and a little rain never hurt anyone, as long as they had their rubber boots and wearing their rain gear, carrying their umbrellas. The Sunday school Sheila use to teach at wasn't too far from the Cartwright school; it was also called Cartwright Sunday school. Sheila use to teach the younger children there, she had a small class room out back of the church area with two or three long tables set up for coloring and reading about the Lord.

When Blossom went to Sunday school, she was so proud to be in her sister's classroom; Sheila would sometimes give Blossom a little extra help in her Sunday school assignments for the day. At this point in Blossom's life she was fitted for glasses, since she had such a high degree of astigmatism. Astigmatism is where the optical in the horizontal plane focus at a distance different from those entering in the vertical plane. Later on Blossom was to discover that she was born with a cataract in her left eye, a cataract is in the lens of the eye where the lens of the eye becomes progressively opaque. Early in the development of a cataract the patient notices a reduction in the acuteness of vision. As the cataract progresses the vision continues to fail until she can perceive the difference between light and darkness, there are different types of cataracts. There was one time though, when we were all walking to school in the middle of winter and there was still snow and ice all over the ground, very wet and slippery, Sheila, Blossom and Cynthia had just finished crossing that busy highway, it was a very cold morning, Blossom missed her footing and slipped on the edge of the sidewalk; with lots of cars buzzing by her, she picked up her thermos that had fallen out of her opened lunch kit, but luckily it hadn't broken, all her sisters were ahead of her and all that they could say was, "hurry up! Blossom," not one came to help her pick up her scattered lunch from the wet ground or even help her up, they were just worried about being late for school.

As they all kept on walking, Blossom quickly picked up her lunch and then ran to catch up. She knew how lucky she was that she hadn't broken her thermos and lost her medication that morning. Blossom was still in grade two at the time, since she had failed the year before. Cynthia had now caught up to her in School, and was now in the same room this term as Blossom.

Blossom's sisters were always smarter that she ever was, most of the time Cynthia would make fun of Blossom, the way younger kids always do, but Blossom knew that she didn't understand her illness. Blossom had to watch that she never got too excited about anything; and she was a very excitable child. If Blossom had gotten too excited she would have one of those seizures, which were more common known as petit-mal. When ever that happened, Cynthia would make fun of the way she acted during one of her seizures, instead of trying to help Blossom out of it. Dawn would always accuse Blossom of starting any argument that would arise from Cynthia's fun making of Blossom, at least to

Blossom in those days it seamed that way, so things got too rough for Blossom to handle she would either take a long walk by herself or have a good father to daughter talk with Casey.

Casey was a quiet man, but very understanding, Blossom could always talk to her father about anything that she couldn't talk to her mother about, like her feelings; for example, Her Mother would always laugh or make a joke of her true feelings when she tried to explain them to Dawn. Dawn always was trying to get Blossom to do better in school, just like any mother would try to do, but when Blossom did what she thought was her best, Dawn wouldn't believe her, she didn't believe a lot of what Blossom ever said back then, just like the very first time she had a seizure, Dawn didn't believe her then. Dawn would say, "Cynthia got better marks then you on her report card," Why can't you? "You are older than she," So Cynthia and Sheila would get maybe a dime or a quarter and Blossom would be left out again. You see in special classes the markings of the report cards were done in a different way, Blossom was in one of those special classes. She was determined that some day she would be out of the special class that she hated so much. It was the beginning of special classes and the teachers didn't want to teach the special children.

Back to the report card markings, the way they marked the report cards were with numbers and not lettering system they have now. The way that system worked was the lower the number the better you were doing in class, but numbering system didn't not mean it was a high as the lettering system, this style of report card markings were only done for the children in special classes, so that they wouldn't feel so bad when the report card time came around. Blossom's report card usually read number one or two. There was one other time when Blossom was in grade two still, she was walking home from school with one of the neighbor boys who lived three houses down from the Cartwright's on Robin Street, he was in the same grade and room as Blossom, this was in the beginning of winter when the snow had just began to fall, they were maybe four houses away from Blossom's home on the way home from school smoking a cigarette, Trent the neighbor boy had stolen them from his sister, who was about twenty at the time. While they were busy smoking acting like grown ups, Trent and Blossom didn't see Dawn, she happened to be standing by the living room window which you could see down the street for a fair distance; she was watching for the children to come home from school, when she saw then walking down the street smoking, she was horrified; Blossom and Trent were trying to keep warm, Blossom didn't know at the time that her mother had seen them, thinking that she hadn't been seen. Blossom had quickly put out her cigarette before entering the driveway, but in the mean time Dawn had seen, and was furious with her. When Blossom had gone inside the house that afternoon, Dawn gave her the lecture and spanking of her entire life, then sent her to her bedroom upstairs with out any dinner.

Dawn never bothered to wait until Casey would come home from work first, when there was punishment to be given out; she would give it to them then. She would of course let Casey know about the crime and punishment later after he had finished eating his dinner and had rested with his newspaper for a bit. Blossom Said, "She thanks her mother to this day for stopping her from ever really starting to smoke back then. Sheila was staying at a girl friends home after school, it was a Friday. Blossom remembers that because she was upset that there was no school the next day, she has always loved to learn new things. Sheila had telephoned to ask if she could stay over the night with her girl friend, Dawn agreed to let her, and proceeded to neatly pack a change of clothing to bring to Sheila later that afternoon. Sheila was old enough then to be trusted out with a girl friend over night. On the way down to drop the clothes off, Dawn remembered that they were out of bird seed for Sheila's budgie bird named Ricky, who later turned out to be a female instead of a male bird, as they had thought they had bought, anyway that was another story. It was getting late and Dawn knew she wouldn't have enough time to pick up the bird seed and take the clothing to Sheila too, Sheila was across town by now. Dawn had wanted to be putting dinner on the table when Casey arrived home that evening. Since they were going right pass the Cartwright school, that wasn't too far from the drug store, Dawn dropped Cynthia and Blossom off to pick up the bird seed, she kept little Willette in the car with her. Blossom was never aloud to go anywhere without one of her sisters tagging along; this time it was Cynthia who was to be her guardian, Cynthia use to hate having to go with Blossom. Dawn had told them both several times to be sure that they heard her, just go in the store and buy the bird seed and then wait until she had came back for them. She said it would be about twenty minutes or so. Well an hour had passed and it was getting darker and darker and then began to rain, they only wore a sweater and no coat, since neither one of them had a an umbrella to go under they decided to start walking home, both Cynthia and Blossom knew their way home since they had walked that route so many times before to school. By this time they both were pretty soaked and scared in the pitch dark, but they knew enough to stay in the lighted areas on the way home. The street was pretty well lit then. As they were walking home a blue and white pickup truck had been following them, then pulled up beside them and stopped. When Blossom turned around to see who it was, she recognized the truck as belonging to her father, they were both so happy to see him they just hopped gladly into the cab of the truck and went home. By the time they were maybe an hour home, the phone rang, being Blossom the closes to the phone, on the wall in the hallway by the kitchen door near the stairs, it was a split level stair case, one set to the basement and one set went up stairs to the bedrooms, she answered the phone, It was a friend of Casey's who was also a friend of the family, he had seen Dawn and Willette in a car accident, the two of them were all right there're in the general hospital, just a little bruises and mostly shaken up from it all. The doctor was going to be releasing them both soon and would Casey please come and pick them up. Casey quickly scooted Cynthia and Blossom over to the neighbors while he drove as tired as he was to pick up Willette and Dawn Since the kids hadn't had anything to eat since noon, Mrs. Smith, who was a well acquainted with the Cartwright family, a grey haired little elderly lady, fixed them up with some chicken noodle soup and a glass of milk. "The old saying marriages are made in Heaven," was true between Casey and Dawn, In the car accident the fellow that hit Dawn diagonally was put into hospital, he had landed in the ditch in such a way that he managed to break a lot of his bones, including the collar bone and right leg.

His son which at the time was a lawyer, and a crafty one at that, came down to the Cartwright's home; one evening to ask to speak to Dawn, "Blossom can still recall the puzzled look on my mother's face before she knew what he had come for. When Dawn finally welcomed him into their home, he threw all kinds of questions at her, one right after the other in connection with the accident until Casey finally had to ask him to leave. Dawn was too smart of women to give him too many answers without her lawyer present first. After a week or two, on one sunny afternoon Dawn was presented that day with a summons at their home, to appear in court in one weeks time from the day she had received the summons.

When the day finally came after what had seemed to Dawn as the longest week in history, Casey decided along time ago that he was going with Dawn to court to give her moral support. He had arranged for time off that afternoon before; to be with his wife in her time of need, the lawyer of the injured party had put Dawn through the mill, trying to twist everything she had told the court. The time came that the lawyer had finished questioning everyone in connection with the accident, it had proved that the injured party had hit Dawn's car he was in fault for speeding while passing in an intersection when it was unsafe to do so. The driver had to pay for Dawn's and Willette's injuries as well as any damages on Dawn's car and all the court costs to boot. It took her years before she ever attempted to drive into town by herself. The accident happened on River Road, Willette was only three at the time, she had the prettiest long ash blonde hair, it was so shinny it use to shine just like golden color of straw when the sun would shine down on it; out back of the chicken coup. At home Willette would ride her little baby blue and white kiddy car, it was the kind you peddle low to the ground, and she would ride it up and down the black top driveway. Sometimes Blossom would give her a little push to get her started down their driveway.

On Robin Street the Cartwright's use to have a large collie dog, one day they decided that they would have to give that dog away, the reason was entirely the postman's fault, thought Blossom. You see the postman use to be afraid of large dogs and would throw stones at her, in return Lassie, that was what we named her would turn on him. One afternoon Lassie bit him after he had hit her with a large stone. "Blossom remembers how she felt when she found out that they were giving her dog away, she was very upset and cried all day, her seizures came all afternoon," It wasn't too long after they purchased the dog that Blossom had decided to give Lassie a bath outside in the corner of the back yard, but first she gave Lassie a large bowl of her favorite dog food and then started to bathe her, Lassie in turn had bit Blossom on her upper right side of her cheek, back then she didn't think that Lassie would mind a bath with her meal," now she laughs about it.

To this day Blossom still has that scar, it has faded some through the years. On the day they gave Lassie away to the young girl who had answered the ad in the newspaper about her dog, she had invited Blossom to come back someday to see Lassie anytime she wanted to, but they never did take Blossom back to see Lassie.

Chapter Two

As A Teenager

After about what might been around eleven years living in the same house, Cartwright's decided to move. Casey had found a parcel of land for sale up on the ridge over looking a Beautiful lake, which in years to come Blossom's grandfather Cartwright would call it a slew, after that the Cartwright's named that beautiful lake Abel's slew as a joke. Well they bought that parcel of land and proceeded in building their new home. Fenton, Dawn's younger brother would come down with his two older sons Paul and Guy to help Casey in the building of their home.

While the house was in progress of being built, the Cartwright's had to move from their home and rent for about six months, Casey found a little white and blue cottage not too far from the Cartwright school, in which the girls could still finish their term in that same school with all their friend. After about a couple of months and in the heat of the summer, Mr. Scott, their landlord came down and asked Dawn's permission for Blossom to sell strawberries for him, this would be in their front yard, so Blossom would have no travel time. Dawn talked it over with Casey and they both agreed that she could work for him, since it would be in the yard out front, there would be always someone to watch her in case of a seizure. After giving their permission Dawn turned and went back into the house cleaning. Mr. Scott then proceeded in where Blossom was playing in the front yard and asked her if she would like to work for him selling baskets of strawberries. Mr. Scott told Blossom that he would pay her for her services a percentage each day. The strawberry stand was set up right out the front of the house near the highway. Oh! Blossom didn't have to worry about transportation since she only had to walk out her front door each morning, then Mr. Scott would bring the berries to her. Blossom always was a hard worker in what ever she would put her mind to. Dawn had told Mr. Scott before hand about Blossom's petit-mal, so not to get her excited and start her seizures going.

As soon as Mr. Scott would bring the berries each morning, Blossom was prepared to start the day with her new job; she was quite thrilled to have that job even though she was only twelve at the time. Sometimes Cynthia would come over to the strawberry stand and try to bribe Blossom from some of her money, but Blossom only gave her some money once from her earnings. Dawn would give Blossom a little jam jar in which she could keep her earnings in each day, then each evening Mr. Scott a kind old grey haired gentleman would come on by to check on how she was doing for the day and pay her. On one occasion he told Blossom that he had another stand about ten miles away, a fifty year old lady was selling there. "Blossom you are doing so much better than she, "Mr. Scott would say with a big grin pasted across his fatherish face.

When Blossom would have a really good day Mr. Scott would give her maybe five dollars more, that was a lot of money back then for a kid, he usually did pay her pretty well. Every night that Blossom got paid, she would go running into the house only after she had properly thanked him first for her earnings in the day. Then show her mother what she had made that day. Dawn had asked Blossom to go put her money in the empty jam jar they had fixed up before hand, she would do this until she had enough saved up in the jar to put into her savings account, that her parents had started for her when she was just a wee babe.

One evening about five-thirty or six o'clock, Blossom was busy as usual with her sales in the berries, with not too many baskets of strawberries left to sell, it had been in the middle of a rush hour traffic, the cars and trucks were bumper to bumper traveling slower than a snail's pace in the heat of the late afternoon. She was hoping to sell out that day to make a good impression for Mr. Scott, Blossom knew that he would be coming On the opposite side of the highway from Blossom's stand. In an old black car there was a middle age man that had asked Blossom how much for the basket of strawberries, they were five pound baskets; If she would bring a basket over to the car he would buy it, since he didn't want to get out of line in the traffic, as he may never get back in again, Blossom understood, she thought about it and decided she would help him out by bringing the basket over to him, in turn he paid the dollar for them After that, she went about three car lengths up, across from the driveway to cross back over. Blossom couldn't see what was coming on the other side of the yellow van. Thinking about the situation she decided to ask the man on the passenger side of the van if there were any cars coming. The younger man must not have understood her, as he told her "No". Blossom then proceeded to cross the busy highway, ran out from behind the stopped car, in front of the yellow van that almost caused Blossom to loose her life, the black sedan had come about one inch from having the front passenger wheel connecting with the top of Blossom's right heel.

After the screeching of the cars and the horrible commotion from the neighbors coming over to see what had just happened, Blossom had then began to get real sacred and have more seizures, those seizures had lasted long into the evening.

That was the last time Blossom ever crossed the busy highway just to sell strawberries, and to this day she said, "I am still afraid of busy highways to cross by self."

At the same place there was another time when Blossom and Cynthia had gone next door to see Mr. Galloway, being a friendly elderly fellow, he worked for a large company with a department store, Mr. Galloway was making wooden toys in his garage that would be latter hand painted by himself and his wife. He would be doing this kind of work out in his garage every evening, he loved children and animals, they had a little terrier pup which was tied on a line from the garage to the driveway, his name was Corky. Cynthia and Blossom would go over some evenings just to watch him in his toy making, he liked to have the children around him when he was making toys, Mrs. Galloway a grey haired motherish type lady would usually bring some home made cookies to the girls, but this time it was around eight o'clock in the evening the girls had asked if they could please pet Corky, Blossom loved animals no matter what kind they were.

Blossom was asked first if she would like to pet Corky while Mr. Galloway was holding him in his lap, as Blossom was the older of the two and very eager to pet Corky, she had brought her hand up too fast to pet him, Corky managed to bite her and nearly took off her whole index finger. Mrs. Galloway went running into the older style farm house from her garden in which she had been busy weeding, she bandaged Blossom's finger temporarily until she could see a doctor.

After those happenings she had seizure after seizure for about one straight week, those individuals' happenings all happened about nineteen-sixty. The Cartwright's then moved from the rented cottage to their brand new home the following summer. Casey had built that home with pride, just like the one before; Dawn would do the interior decorating. Sometimes Casey would take Blossom to work with him and she would be able to stay all day with her daddy. One day Casey got a hold of a very good contract; they had to have some large machinery out digging the foundation hole to begin the building. Casey would have to leave his Blossom home with the rest of the girls, when he did take her, she would help nail, usually she missed the two by tens to nail the floor to, but then she would help by carrying the small pieces of wood cuttings out to the burning pile. By lunch time Casey and Blossom would find a couple of short, but not too short boards, usually plywood and set them up against the wall for back rests, those boards would rest on a forty-five degree angle slope so that it was comfortable, this was while eating their lunch that Dawn had so nicely packed earlier that morning. Sometimes Dawn would put cabbage in the tomato sandwich instead of lettuce, that was when Casey would threw out the cabbage and not mention it to her.

On the occasions that he would take Blossom to work with him, she was very excited to be with her daddy, but he had to be so careful that she didn't have a seizure and fall into a pile of burning scrapes or a large hole that had just been freshly dug. Blossom looked forward in the days that she could be with her daddy at work, you see he treated her like he would treat any of the other three daughter, not a special case and Blossom like that.

This was a Sunday afternoon the sun was shinning and Dawn just wanted to go for a drive, she really didn't want to go and visit; but Casey decided that they should and they did. As soon as they had gotten there, Blossom's cousin Guy who was much younger, asked her to come up in the attic and see the new baby Robins in their nest. Blossom didn't want to go up to the attic, but Dawn told her that she would enjoy seeing the baby Robins. She didn't want to hurt Guy's feelings so she went, she was the last of the four kids to go up, Cynthia, Willette were right behind Guy. You see Blossom knew that the adults wanted to talk without kids hanging around. While Blossom was walking on the floor of the unfinished attic, she Happened to step on the gyp rock; the two by fours laying across the gyp rock in which they had to cross to get to the nest. After slipping off the two by fours and onto the gyp rock; Blossom fell through the ceiling and into the living room about one yard away from their chesterfield. Everyone came running just to see what the crash was all about and then Casey and Jake, Fenton's brother-in-law helped Blossom to one of the bedrooms down the hall, as she couldn't walk by herself. There Dawn and Aunty Mae, Fenton's wife took a look at her hip, it had been hurting her very much at the time. Then about what seemed to be a long time to Blossom, Casey and Dawn decided to take Blossom home. Jake helped Casey again with Blossom to the car, one of Blossom's arms, around her daddy, and the other arm around Jake's neck as she hobbled out, to the back seat of the car. In the blue Chevy Blossom sat with her leg on the seat resting it, while her sisters were sitting up front, Sheila didn't come that day, being a Sunday and Dawn not really believing that Blossom couldn't walk on her leg, thinking she only sprained it. She put Blossom to bed as soon as they reached the house, but not before she lectured her on her behavior and was made to try and stand on her leg first. That night was a night-mare for Blossom and Casey; since Casey had to help her to the bathroom and she couldn't sleep because of the pain in her hip. The next morning Casey decided to take time off work to take Blossom to see a doctor, it was old Doc. Wade, his office was way across town with about twenty-five steps to climb straight up, but Casey and Dawn managed together to get Blossom up to the top to his office. Doctor Wade then examined Blossom's leg and sent her back down the stairs; the same way she got up with her parents help, it was hard on her parents both hanging onto her waist. Blossom had to be taken to a hospital that was quite a few miles away from the office; it was quite a struggle for them as they were getting on in their years. They had to make sure that Blossom hadn't blacked out or she would be falling down the stairs; taking them with her. After that day old Doc. Wade had relocated his office to a new location on a main floor. Apparently Blossom had broken her right hip, where most elderly people would break it. Casey and Dawn had managed to get her back into the car to the hospital down the street.

In time to come Casey was to find that they had no room left on the children's ward for his Blossom. From there Blossom was transported on a stretcher by three ambulance attendance, one at the head supporting the head, one supporting her back and the other supporting her legs, Being careful not to bend the legs, on the count of three they all lifted Blossom at the same time. Blossom was then transported in the ambulance, Dawn was sitting up front with one of the attendance, while she was giving him the details on how it all happened, Dawn would be looking back every so often to see how Blossom was doing, Casey and the three girls were following in the old Chevy. That was when Blossom had told the young attendant who was in the back with her, she had wished that she could have a ride in a ambulance while they were going to her Uncle's home, and now her wish had come true. The Young Attendant then helped Blossom to sit up a little so she could wave to her father and sisters, which was a great moment for Blossom.

Well Blossom was taken to the general hospital for children, that afternoon, the sun was shinning and the birds were singing in the trees above. When she finally arrived at the hospital a nurse and Dawn escorted her to the children's ward, Dawn drew the hospital curtains while Blossom was changing out of her play clothes into one of those hospital gowns, you know the type, the uncomfortable ones that only do up half way in the back. That children's ward had only two empty beds left. At first the doctors examined her leg; again the doctors had a discussion in which way to heal the broken bone the fastest. First they put her leg in traction and was going to let the break heal on it's own, but that was going to take too long a time, then the doctors decided that they would put her leg in a cast, that would cover the whole leg, but that was going to take too much wrapping and would be way too uncomfortable for Blossom in the heat of the summer. It took three days and nights with Blossom's leg in traction, before the doctors decided to operate on her hip and put the stainless steel pin in, they had the pin screwed to her bone. In the operating room the doctors and nurses all wore white gowns and masks that just covered their mouth and nose. In the actual operating there was first a surgeon, although the surgeon is the important figure he does not work alone. He is the head of the team that; preformed Blossom's operation. A second doctor acted as the first assistant, then there was what you call scrub nurses; they handle the instruments in the room, last but not least there was a circulating nurse, she moves in and out of the room as a liaison between the operative field and the sterilizing supplies. You must be wondering by now how a young girl like Blossom knew all this about their procedures, well I'll tell you; just before she went under anesthesia The nurse made her count backwards from one hundred, in that way they knew when the anesthesia was working. The recovery room was a fairly small room with maybe only two beds and an experienced nurse to look after her. Casey, and Dawn, were patiently waiting for when Blossom would be coming out of the recovery room, both of them always would come to visit Blossom every day while she was laid up in that hot stuffy hospital. Dawn had brought her the stuffed brown dog she called Toasty, it was her favorite of all her toys, the dog had long floppy ears and a tail that had been sewn up about twenty times or more, as the days went on, there was one evening when all the other children were fast asleep, Blossom couldn't sleep since it was so hot in there, it had given her a headache, she rang for the night nurse who happened to be a slender elderly lady, you know the grandmother type. Blossom asked her for an aspirin for her headache, she use to get real bad migraines from the heat, but since she was on other medication for her petit-mal she couldn't mix the medication with ones for her headache without the doctor's ok at that time of night, he was sure to be home in bed by then, since he had an early, morning operation to perform the next day The very next best thing the nurse could think of was to bring a plastic bag of ice cubes and put that on her head, it would take the pressure of the heat away and lesson her pain, that headache was just jawing at her head. Come morning Blossom's bed was full of water, just soaked through from the ice bag leaking in the night. She was then put on a large padded arm chair by her bed to sit while the chamber maids came and remade her bed with clean fresh sheets. About two weeks after, Casey had gone down town and bought Blossom a pair of crutches to learn how to walk all over again, before she was able to use the crutches, she had to learn how to walk in a walker, they are much like a walker for small children only much larger. The walker had a seat so that when she had gotten tired of walking she could sit and rest awhile. Blossom and another lady use to walk in the metal walkers up and down the hallways together. The wooden crutches were rough on the top under the arms, where the arm pits would touch, so Casey got out some underlay felt that he had left over from a rug on one of the houses he had just finished building. Casey would then put the under lay felt on top and wrap it with masking tape to protect her under arms from being rubbed raw by the wooden crutches. The nurses would teach Blossom how to walk in the hospital up and down the stairs near the side entrance where there wasn't much traffic from people coming in and out; Blossom learned fast and was pretty good on them. When it was time to go home her parents came to pick her up in their fairly new air conditioned car. Blossom had made quite a few friends in her stay in the hospital. On Blossom's way out she hobbled over to say good-bye to Mark, he had the same thing wrong with his leg as she did, but they left him in traction to heal on it's own.

Mark and Blossom became good friends while in the hospital, she use to go over and sit down in the arm chair by his bed side and they would play cards together, Blossom knew that he cheated a lot, but she didn't want to hurt his feelings by telling him so.

It was a beautiful sunny afternoon and every one was happy to see Blossom back home again, even Cynthia was very happy that day to see Blossom. That summer was one of Blossom's summers that she was going to remember for a long time to come, she had to exercise her right leg every day by lifting two five pounds sand bags that Casey had made especially from the doctors requirements. Blossom use to sit in front of the broom cupboard in the kitchen on a yellow chair with a straight back while the whole family would be cheering her on, sometimes they would try it too. Just to see how long they could lift their leg with a five pound sand bag tied in the middle to hang on either side of their leg. For Blossom to get the vitamin "C" she needed to help heal her leg she was to be given two to three oranges per day. Periodically Blossom would have to go for a check-up, the doctor would say to Blossom "you're coming along fine," This was a specialist, not doctor Wade. "Blossom could still remember waiting in the little cubical room they have for patients to go in while examining them, her mother would say, "Well! Blossom which door do you think he will be coming through today," there was two doors to that room, one from the hallway and one from the waiting room, that was a little game Blossom and Dawn use to play to pass the time while waiting for him.

Blossom was thirteen then, she recalls the time when she was still in the hospital and she was aloud to sit by this one's girls bed while eating supper, the kitchen staff had made mashed potatoes with green parsley on top, peas and a slice of white bread for all the children for dinner that night, the meat was turkey, Blossom didn't really like potatoes no matter how they were cooked, so she wasn't upset when the young girl swung around on her bed and accidentally stuck her bare feet in Blossom's mashed potatoes. About half an hour before visiting time, was when that all happened, then just before the visiting time was to end, the night nurse would bring around a tea wagon filled with apple juice and baby cookies, some time there was orange juice for the children, once in awhile if there was enough the visitors got some too. Blossom still likes her baby cookies and apple juice to this day. By the time school was back in session, Blossom, Cynthia and Willette would get a ride to and from school, Dawn would drive them and pick them up again, Shelia was in high school by then. As Blossom was still on crutches there wasn't too much walking or many sports she was able to do for a long time to come.

Blossom liked sports; Cynthia liked the idea of getting a ride to and from school, not that Blossom and Willette didn't. Blossom was in occupational class at the time she broke her leg, it was considered as grade seven then, in junior high school the occupational class wasn't just for children that had learning disabilities or for dummies like most people thought they were back then, it was for children who were slower than the ones in the regular classes. Sometimes when Blossom was coming down the junior high school stairs on her crutches, there were two sets of fairly wide stairs from the top floor in which they had to travel in order to get to one class, then the bell would ring to be in your class, but Blossom was excused if she was late for any class on the account she was slower with her crutches than the rest of them who didn't have crutches. There would be this one girl that would help her carry her brief-case after the bell had rang, so not to get into trouble for being late, Blossom knew that was the only reason she would help her out, "Now! Don't get me wrong," Blossom would say, the girls in the school didn't hate me. I just found it harder than most teenagers to make friends with other girls. Blossom was on crutches for most of the year, then gradually with the doctors help Blossom was able to walk on her own again. When Blossom was growing up, living in the new house on the ridge, there was a lot of happenings going on. Blossom was walking up the steep hill on her way home from school, this fellow, about in his thirties in a black sedan car pulled up to Blossom, he was wearing a pair of black curled up at the toe fairly good dress shoes and a black suit as if he was going to a funeral, he had asked Blossom about an address and since she didn't know where it was she said so, went on her way leaving him to go on his, at least she thought he had until Blossom had reached her home that afternoon and the same car was parked in the driveway. He was in the back yard with Willette and her little girl friend she had brought home with her from school that afternoon. Casey and Dawn happened to be at a friends funeral at the time, so of course the doors were all locked up, but the house had a shed that was attached to the basement part in the carport and the key was inside the door. "Thank God!" said Blossom that we were always taught never to let any stranger into the house for any reason. On that afternoon when Blossom had arrived home and recognized that it was the same car that had stopped her on the hill earlier, she knew right away something was very wrong. He had the girls try and look for a window open or an unlocked door to get into the house. Willette, Blossom and the little girl friend being too smart and scared from his bluffs, sneaked around the back side of the house and pretended to be looking for the key or an opened window, when all they were doing was stalling for time to think of their next move to make Blossom wanted Willette to go over to the neighbors for help, but she was too afraid that he might see her and catch them then hurt them. Blossom knew that when she got too excited she wouldn't make any since and they might not understand what she would be trying to say. The neighbors Blossom decided to see lived across the graveled road behind the large trees, they were retired school teachers. Blossom saw the husband outside in his garden, he was a fabulous gardener, anyway she went over to him and tried to tell him, but Blossom figured that he didn't really understand what she trying to say as she kept looking over her shoulder to see if Willette and her friend were still ok. She didn't want to leave Willette and her girl friend alone too long with that guy.

When Blossom was coming back home through the driveway entrance, she spotted Cynthia and trying to warn her not to come into the yard, but as usual Cynthia knew everything and just pushed her way past Blossom, wouldn't even listen to what she had to say at all, as if that was some sort of a game and she wasn't going to be left out.

Blossom said, "I guess Cynthia thought that she might be missing something if she didn't come into the back yard to see what was going on. That fellow he tried to pump them for information on their family, like knowing how many are in the family and when they will be back home, you know little things that would add up to a lot in the end. Blossom tried everything she knew how not to tell him the truth about anything, but good old Cynthia not taking heed to Blossom's warnings she went straight ahead and told him everything he wanted to know, which in return he knew that Blossom was just playing games with him. That fellow had tried to pump for all sorts of information, by Cynthia doing what he asked she almost got herself into a lot of trouble not to mention her sisters too, right there in the back yard with only one neighbor to be home. He had tried to get them to give him a massage on the patio, plus what ever else he could dream up, "Thank God!" Cynthia finally came to her senses and didn't go along with him anymore. Blossom suggested that he go see one of the neighbors, an adult, but he told them that he didn't like grown-ups very much. Blossom recalls," the way his shoes curled way up on the toe part like a pixie's shoe. He finally got scared enough and went on his way. That evening Casey and Dawn phoned the police, straight away they came out, Edger and Peggy, the retired school teachers that Blossom had gone to see earlier for help; felt real sick when they found out what Blossom was trying to tell them earlier, Edgar and Peggy came over to apologize to the girls for not understanding Blossom before hand. The police questioned Cynthia and Blossom being the elder of the three that were involved in it. Blossom was sitting in the green rocking chair that squeaked when it rocked feeling kind of scared and relieved all at the same time, while Cynthia was seated near her parents on the chesterfield across the room from Blossom, just gloating away about the whole episode. Blossom figured that the police didn't really believe them and to this day she hadn't heard weather or not if they had caught the fellow. There was a different time when Blossom was still on crutches that Cynthia had tried to hurt her quite a bit, like the time that Blossom was standing with her crutches in the hallway by the staircase, Blossom had just come out of a seizure and was coming aware of her surroundings again, when Cynthia tried to push her down the stairs, she had been in a bad mood that day and was taking it out on Blossom as usual. The day before Cynthia had just grabbed Blossom's crutches from underneath her arms while she was struggling to come up the basement stairs from the den where the TV was located, Cynthia would always do things like that when Dawn or Casey weren't around watching. Then you see she can deny any accusations made by Blossom and they would think that Blossom was just making up stories again. While Blossom was still going to junior high school there was quite a few boys who liked her and use to walk her home from school sometimes. This one boy from her class named Virgil, he was a little on the slow side, because of his speech problems, Virgil had brought a box of Valentine chocolates to school in a brown paper bag, like a lunch bag, On Valentine day on his way home from school he had left out the back way so he could catch up to Blossom walking up the steep hill on her way home, that afternoon Virgil wanted to give her the Valentine chocolates; only Blossom's hand were filled with books to study, she had wanted in the worse way to get out of the occupational class. Blossom couldn't take the lovely box of chocolates from him, so Virgil had taken the brown paper bag which contained the Valentine chocolates and putted on top of her books; Blossom, she had thought that it was his old lunch bag, that he was playing some sort of a trick on her, so when she had told him that she didn't want his old lunch bag, Virgil quickly took out the beautiful wrapped Valentine box of chocolates with a tiny yellow and black bumble bee mounted on the top of the fancy wrapped box, Virgil had wrapped it very carefully himself the night before. At first Blossom was very flattered that he wanted to give her a lovely box of Valentine chocolates, but she thought for awhile as they continued to walk up the steep hill, Blossom very tactfully said that she couldn't accept the box of chocolates right now, she knew that what she was about to say next would probably hurt his feelings, that was the last thing she wanted to do, but she was taught not to accept anything under false pretence. Very politely Blossom refused the box of chocolates for the reason that she had her eyes on someone else and he didn't even know that she was alive. Virgil had insisted that she keep the chocolates anyway and since her arms were filled with books she had no other choice. When Blossom had arrived home that afternoon Casey and Dawn both teased her about the box of chocolates until she had enough teasing and started into her seizures again, Yes Blossom had gotten too excited one more time and started her blackouts. The very next day in class the girls apparently had known all about the incident that had taken place with Virgil that afternoon before, they had really put Blossom on the spot by asking her why she didn't like Virgil. After that day he never walked home with Blossom again, "I guess you could say he finally got the message, but he did have such respect for her. Blossom always had lots of boy friends at school, a couple of days later John walked Blossom up that same steep hill until she was able to get him to go on his way home before he would get into trouble from his older sister for not returning straight home after school, You see he lived with his older sister. There! was one boy however that Blossom had a crush on, he use to play his guitar on the bus when ever the class went on a outing, all the girls use to crowd around him just to hear him sing, What!

Beautiful singing voice he had, remembered Blossom as she leaned back in her rocker one more time. Mark McCarthy, he was called; she could remember it just as if it had happened yesterday. Mark was the handsome young fellow in her classroom, you know the type tall dark and handsome, with big brown eyes and long black eyelashes.

Mark's baby face would make you want to melt right into his loving arms. His body was the perfect slender body any young man could ever wish for. One time Blossom had brought all her stamps that she had been collecting for along time to school and gave them all to Mark, while he was standing at his locker next to hers.

She was too shy to give them to him in the classroom, because she thought that the girls would make fun of her crush on Mark. That was the only thing that Blossom couldn't cope with, the fact that they would make fun of something that was so dear to her heart. So she gave them to Mark in hopes that he might add them to his stamp collection he had at home and then maybe he would want to get to know her better. Blossom thought that maybe he might even ask her out for a date once or twice, but to her surprise Mark just thanked her and went on his way, that was the last attention he ever paid to Blossom. The old saying, "you can't buy love sure is true," thought Blossom. Eventually she just gave up on him, since he still wasn't showing any interest in her by the end of the year.

Mark had brought his white stallion horse to school and tied him up to a tree in the back, having the horse there was creating so much confusion with the children in the classroom that he had to remove his horse at lunch hour. He did how ever let Blossom and some of the other kids pet his horse, which was a very excitable day for her, she did however manage to control her excitement so not to have too many seizures.

Chapter Three

Sheila's Wedding

It was now about nineteen-sixty-four and the year that Sheila becomes Mrs. Grant Williams. Sheila had asked Blossom to be her maid of honor at the alter on her wedding day, Blossom was quite excited about being asked, since her greatest wish was to be Sheila's maid of honor someday.

Since she was so excited about being the maid of honor Blossom had nothing but seizures after seizure. You see Blossom would say, she wasn't suppose to get overly excited too often even at times now that she was becoming less frequent with seizures. Well! Dawn had heard about that and she soon put a stop to it, she decided to decline for Blossom from the offer, since she was afraid that Blossom might have a seizure while standing at the alter.

The week before the wedding was to take place, she had went out on a date with one of Grant's boarders; who just so happened to be a police officer at the time. Sheila had asked Blossom before hand not to say anything to Grant about her date, "to this day Blossom hadn't said a word about it to him.

Mr. William Sr. had been drinking for a long time now, his drinking problem was now starting to break up his marriage. He worked in a small news paper firm, in the press department, "they have three sons no daughters, Blossom would go on to say." At the day of the wedding, a beautiful ceremony it was in the church not far from home, Mr. Williams sat alone at the back pew crying. The reception was by seven in the evening at the Royal Canadian Legion, just down from the church in behind a beautiful garden of evergreens. Sheila wore a beautiful full length gown in white of sheer over taffeta and lace, with lily-point sleeves. The something old she wore was her mother's veil she had been married in many years prior, it was now fashioned in shoulder length and was held in place by a pearl tiaras. Sheila carried a cascade bouquet of white carnations and yellow roses. The maid of honor was an old school friend; Sheila had been chumming around with and was friends for a long time after. The bride's maid were her cousins, both the bridesmaids and maid of honor wore identical dresses of deep pink satin, tiaras crowned their heads and carried cascades bouquets of white carnations and deep pink roses. The flower girl was Willette, she was demure in white, and flower girl dress was fashioned by Dawn and was accented by a deep pink cummerbund. Willette wore a tiara of seed pearls and carried a tiny nosegay of white carnations and deep pink rose buds. Best man was Joe Donaldson of the United States a friend of the Williams family, while the ushers were two cousins of Grant's also from the United States. Grant's aunt was standing in for his mother, she wore an ensemble of blue brocade with pink accessories, Grant's father wore a grey suit with a white carnation in the lapel Dawn wore a suit of beige brocade and both wore corsages of pink and white carnations After the wedding services were all over they went down to the studio for photo pictures and then reception was ready to start. Toast to the bride was given by her Uncle Fenton. For their honeymoon trip Sheila wore a suit of pink brocade with white accessories and a corsage of white rose buds. She wore a blue garter belt around her left leg near the knee; then when the time came, Grant had the honor of taking it off and throwing the blue garter in the traditional way with all the unattached gentlemen lined up behind him to catch the garter.

In the next seven months they gave birth to a beautiful bouncing baby boy, which they named Sheldon. Sheldon was born the very same day that Blossom's Grandfather Cartwright was buried. Since they lived so far away Casey took Blossom and Cynthia on the train with him to the funeral, so they were not around when the news came in that Sheldon was born into this world of bewilderment. You see Grandfather Cartwright lived on the prairies and it took three days by train in order to get to their destination on time. Being Christmas time Dawn had packed some turkey sandwiches for their trip. Sometimes they would buy their meals on the train, since they were getting tired of turkey sandwiches. Casey and the two girls managed to arrive two days before the time for the funeral services. Marcy, Casey's cousin's girl friend was also there, it had been a sad time for everyone.

Blossom had to make sure those days that she had taken her medication while the rest of the family had gone to the services, then off to the cemetery, Marcy took Cynthia and Blossom out for a ride in the car while the services were going on. The three of them stayed for a couple of days and then left back on the train for home. Grandmother Cartwright made some more turkey sandwiches for them to take on the long trip back with them. To Casey's and the girls surprise after being cooped up and late on the train coming home, which turned out to be about three hours late that evening, after helping a derailed passenger train back all the way up to the station in which they had just left three hours before. Dawn had a beautiful twenty pound turkey all cooked with all the trimmings for the three of them waiting for their arrival home. By the time they finally had arrived, it was eight o'clock in the evening and the turkey was well over done. Casey and the girls never wanted to be so rude by refusing the beautiful turkey dinner, but they took one look at that turkey and nearly got sick for having nothing but turkey for the last week. With that in mind Casey took everyone out for a hamburger that evening, the next day they all sat down to the beautiful turkey dinner. By nineteen sixty-six Blossom had started to write in a diary, on the first day of January the Cartwright's had a huge New Years party in their basement that lasted until two-ten in the morning with almost all their relatives still there.

The following day Blossom spent a quiet day at home with her family, in the evening Blossom finished reading a book that she had started about a week ago, she never was a fast reader, this book was called flower of the jungle. That book was about the young girl who had gotten lost in the jungle and how the natives had discovered her and raised her up to be one of their own. By the third day from the party, Blossom was still recuperating from the loss of sleep. She did most of sleeping during that day while it was quiet in the house. Sheila and Grant were busy with their new baby now, they didn't want too much company those days, so Blossom felt kind of lost at what to do.

Chapter Four

Blossom's Diary

On January Fourth; Blossom writes Cynthia, Willette and herself started home form school that morning, there was a blizzard warning out for people to stay inside their homes, she noticed that the grounds were covered with snow and the school had all ready been shut down for the day. Blossom didn't really mind, since she hadn't been feeling too well that morning. Blossom had quite a few stomach cramps; she was shocked to discover that this was the time she was to start into womanhood. Blossom yelled in fear for her mother, Dawn came running to see what the matter was; when she found out Dawn just gave her a pad and showed her how to use it, and told her there was nothing to worry about.

The next day it rained all day, she wrote in her tiny blue diary, there was still quite a bit of snow on the grounds; Blossom had managed to catch a terrific cold in the morning, so she wasn't feeling well the rest of the day.

By January ninth; Blossom hadn't entered anything in her diary, her cold kept her from doing much of anything. She was in bed for most of those days. Blossom was still in occupational class, their family had moved to a new home at the top of a hillside, she was now working on a job study program; that particular day being a school day, Blossom was working in the school office again. She really liked office work, but that day the principal had decided that she should go home early, Blossom hadn't been feeling too well all day, Blossom was blacking out most of the day. When Casey arrived home late that afternoon from a hard day of working in construction. Blossom was fast asleep, hadn't even wanted any dinner. Casey then, decided to go out and feed her animals one being a calf, Blossom had now been raising a white face calf for the past three years. That calf was born from the family milking cow, which was artificially bred, the calf was born in the pasture one sunny afternoon, Casey had to go out to help the mother cow give birth, as she was having trouble with her first calf. The calf was born on a pile of rocks; Willette named him Rocky for that reason.

Eleventh of January Blossom had been thinking strongly about writing a book and getting it published some day. She also thought that the rest of the family was not ready to have a writer in their family as of yet, they didn't take her serious on wanting to write a book. Blossom forgot to write her episodes of the day in her diary, since she had been so excited about writing that book that day, She did mention to me that she had been down town to the corner store buying the materials she needed to get started on the book writing.

On January fourteenth; the William's left that afternoon while Blossom was in school, her class had just gone to a beauty salon with the home economics teacher to have their hair washed and set free. When they had arrived back to school, Blossom had gone straight to work in the school, office.

The next day being a Saturday Blossom went bowling with some of her girl friends in town, she was a pretty good bowler and she enjoyed it very much. Then in the late afternoon she watched a show on the television and fell asleep quickly.

January sixteenth Jenny called, she was one of the twins, came to pick Blossom up after church to go to another young woman friend's home for a birthday party. They had lots of fun and games to play, Lora had received lots of beautiful birthday presents that day; thought Blossom.

January seventeenth, Monday Blossom worked in the school office again writing out names and doing some typing, filling and copy writing, she just loved to work with paper. Blossom also worked on the adding machine and had strung beads for the principal that belonged to a girl. When Blossom got home that afternoon, she had decided to write out an application for a part time typist job in town, for part time work after school.

The very next morning Dawn took Blossom out of school to take her white face calf (Rocky) to an auction sale, Blossom had raised him alone for the past three and half years, now she was ready to sell him. Blossom loved that white face calf very much, but she either had to sell him or Casey would have him butchered for the dinner table. Blossom knew she had to sell her Rocky. The auction was to be held that morning, it turned out that the biding for Blossom's calf wasn't going to be until the next morning.

The next day being January the nineteenth she stayed out of school again to sell her calf. Dawn had taken Blossom to the auction barns that morning to see Rocky one last time, Blossom had a thing about animals, all her animals were to have names before they were to be sold at the auction. That morning Rocky brought in $100.50 and he had weighed in at 400 pounds. That was a lot of money for Blossom back in those days, she said after awhile with a grin pasted across her face.

The next day part of Blossom's lunch had been stolen from her school locker. Later that day she was to find out who had pulled such a dirty trick on her. Blossom was lucky that the thief hadn't stolen her thermos of milk with the medication in it. There were four tranquilizers for her petit-mal placed in her thermos of milk. It turned out to be Abigail Black, her locker partner. In the afternoon Blossom worked in the school office, but in between working in the office, she had a test to write. In her diary Blossom had wrote that they had company for the past two days and that was why she hadn't had the time to get around in writing in her diary again.

January twenty-first, Blossom writes she had talked to the principal, who she was working for, to apply for a job opening she knew was coming up soon. She had been working as a job study in the office for the last two years, when you work as a job study as Blossom had been doing through the school, you don't get paid for it.

It was all part of your learning the program. Blossom said that at first she was quite nervous to go up to the principal and apply for the job as a secretarial position. Unfortunately he turned her down, because of some silly school regulations, that a principal can not hire a student from his school.

There was a boy from China in the class now. He couldn't speak or understand English too well. On the twenty-sixth of January Blossom learned how to say YOUR WELCOME in French, this was how she had said it, 'JE VOUS" EN PRIE,' not bad Hey! Blossom would say with that certain twinkle in her eye.

The following day Blossom was very excited. She had to watch it though; that she would take it easy and not have any seizures on her first date with that handsome looking young guy who was Peter Prescott, a rich tall dark good natured young fellow. The rest of the Cartwright's had gone out to see a movie called "I'll SEE YOU IN HELL DARLING. Before Blossom went out on her date, she had made a salmon casserole and a lemon pie for dinner, her mother wasn't feeling up to cooking, Dawn had been sick most of the day, that was why Casey thought it would be good for Dawn to get out of the house and away from the house cleaning for awhile, Dawn always kept a spotless house. January twenty-nine, Saturday, went bowling with Uncle Jed and Aunt Jill; he had gotten remarried about five years after Cara's death. They then came home and had some tea, watched a little TV and went straight to bed.

What happened on January the thirty-first, a Tuesday, an older girl chum of Blossom's came over, they played records in the bedroom upstairs for the best part of the day. At school everything went wrong for Blossom, from the very first, it was a very drawn out day. By then Grant's family had moved back to the Charlottes area. When February the first rolled around Blossom wrote a letter to her sister Sheila, said that the family would be out to visit them soon, maybe by the twenty-seventh, or the first of March. February Fourth. Dear diary she wrote, Yesterday I went to a beauty parlor and a young French girl gave me a perm in my hair; Blossom was so upset with the way it was done, that she had seizures all day. Yes even a little thing like having her hair done the wrong way could trigger off her black outs then. Blossom's hair had gone all frizzy; she was very fussy about how her hair looked. Since Blossom had done so well in the office before, the principal put her back working at the school office. Later after school when she was home for awhile she had gone out to feed the animals she loved so much, by then they had a cow, and golden Labrador dog, who had to be chained up on a run because Dawn was worried that he might get into the fertilizer and die, a couple of sheep and a horse to look after. Later that same evening all of a sudden while Blossom was in the house, she heard something in the barn, running out to see what it was, the old horse had come barreling out from the barn side door and into the pasture. At that point Blossom started to run and see what had scared her horse so much, while doing so, she had tripped over a rock, then started to black out from all the excitement, apparently she had let herself get so worked up over the horse barreling out, that she had seizures again.

February fifth, Blossom walked all the way into town to take her tiny watch to be repaired, the fellow who owned the place knew Blossom from when she was just a little girl; still living on the ridge. So he repaired the tiny watch for free. His office was located about three miles down the steep hill from the Cartwright's home Blossom would usually walk the distance to get her exercise, she also had some one-twenty film to be processed which was only three doors down on the same side of the street, Blossom liked that, because she didn't like crossing the busy streets by Herself, ever since she was almost ran over selling those strawberries when she was a little girl. The same evening the whole family went bowling with their Aunt and Uncle, Blossom was getting her score pretty well up there by now. Casey was also teaching her how to keep score. The family never went bowling that much, but when they did they would also take Blossom along with them, she really liked it. February sixth, the Cartwright's were invited out to dinner at their Uncle Fenton' home, Dawn's younger brother and wife Mae, they had roast beef and vegetables all ready with the dinner rolls, warming in the oven. That was one thing the Cartwright's always had with their dinners, a slice of bread or dinner roll. After dinner was all over Aunt Mae, Dawn and Blossom had finished the dishes. Blossom was given a single dinner plate from out of Aunt Mae's cupboard, this dinner plate was white with a pale green boarder, the dinner plate use to belong to a dinner set that was Dawn's Mother's. The plate was still in perfectly good condition, it was a part of the set that Hannah received for a wedding gift from; her boss many years ago. Dawn had worked in the same hotel making beds and meals that her mother before her had worked in. By now that single plate was antique, worth a pretty penny. On February eighth; Blossom had put the dinner plate very carefully wrapped in tissue paper in her Grandmother Cartwright's old steam trunk that was made into a hope chest by her dad for, Blossom. Then she went off to school and finished the red jumper that she was working on in home economics class. Later that day, the class was treated to a movie, an educational film in the classroom, called "THE INNOCENT STORY,' on sex. That evening when Blossom had returned home, there was a letter from Sheila waiting for Her, The following day Blossom had quite a few more seizures and after school she stayed for a dance, as they would call them in those days a mixer, a Valentine dance in the gym. She had gotten home around seven that evening from the mixer, with her two sisters, Cynthia and Willette. February twelfth; went bowling again at the Whiteland bowling alleys with some friends, Blossom's average was now one-hundred eighteen. February Thirteenth; some friends of the Cartwright's family came over and stayed for dinner. Then after dinner and the dishes were all cleared away, Hal trimmed the grape vines out back near the strawberry field for Dawn, Hal is a terrific gardener, he is Casey's cousin's husband. The following day Blossom's girl friend came over for awhile; they played records and danced in the recreational room down stairs, then at one-thirty she left. As you can see Blossom's life so far hasn't been too exciting for a young girl. February Fifteen, Dad got his glasses today, while he was in getting them fitted Blossom picked up her pictures from the photographers, she had brought in a week ago, not too many of them turned out, the photographer hadn't charged her anything for the ones that didn't turn out since it was the first time Blossom ever used a camera. February Sixteenth; Wednesday, Blossom was excited about being elected the class representative, On Monday there will be a student counsel meeting. To Blossom that was like being a girl most popular in her class. By the time that she had finally run all the way home that afternoon, Blossom, ended up having more seizures and had to go to her room to rest awhile before she could tell them about her good news. Blossom could just curse those darn seizures every time she would get excited and want to tell the people she loved about her day, she wouldn't make any sense and then soon they just didn't pay any attention to what she said anymore. Blossom was always getting excited about one thing or another, it was very difficult for her not to get too emotional, she had to try and control her excitement so she wouldn't have those seizures so much. By this time the seizures have been slowing down, but only if she could control her excitement.

February Twenty, Blossom had walked down the hill to town and bought a brand new pair of black Swede shoes after school, Marcy came over again late that afternoon. Then at dinner time Casey and Blossom had a big fight. Her father pushed her against the wall from the dinner table and hit Blossom on the nose; she ended up with a bloody nose and was sent to her bedroom without any dinner. All Dawn could say was "don't break her glasses Casey," To this day Blossom still can't figure out what the fight was all about. February Twenty-one,

Tuesday the first part of the day from nine to lunch hour, Blossom spent in the council meeting. Boy! Did it ever feel good to be elected a class rep., thought Blossom while sitting in the meeting.

February Twenty-Third, Nineteen Sixty-Six; Blossom was writing out those recipes from the other day, one of her hobbies collecting recipes. While she was busy writing one of the recipes out, she still was dreaming about Jack, the more he appeared in her mind, the more she thought that she had fallen in love with him.

February twenty-Eight, hadn't written in the diary for a couple of days now. "The class was taken down to the Inn for a full course meal at noon. "Boy!" was it good, "Mrs. Nola took the whole cooking class down, and paid for the whole tab. She was the nicest cooking teacher, a large framed black haired jolly person in addition a smile as big as the outdoors.

March Second, Well Sheila, Grant and their little family of two finally arrived to the Cartwright's again from up North, the little one Betty was now cutting her first tooth, she was really a good baby about it. March THIRD, Sheila, Grant, Blossom, Dawn and Casey all stayed up until eleven in the evening cleaning up after Willette's birthday party, she was seven now. Then watched some TV the show was called, "THE TOWN WITH NO PITY," it was very good, thought Blossom. March Fifth, Blossom's knee gave out while bowling with Sheila and Grant's family, it was the first time her right knee ever gave out on her. March Sixth, went driving through Whiteland Crescent, it was a lovely drive, got to bed at twenty-to ten PM. March eighth, Blossom still wasn't feeling too well today, and she got up at three in that afternoon and fainted right outside the bathroom door. The following day she was still too sick to do anything around the house, so she just mostly stayed in bed.

The next time Blossom wrote in her diary was March Twenty; she only wrote feeling sick diary, "Sorry I didn't keep you up to date." March Twenty-One, Today was the first day of spring, the blossoms still on the apple tree was as beautiful as ever. How ever Blossom still hadn't gotten over the flu, Casey had been quite generous to her that day.

March Twenty-Two, "Blossom finally finished the puzzle that her dad had brought her; the day before when she was still fast asleep, he had brought a piece of plywood so Blossom had something hard to put her puzzle; on while still in bed. Casey had tiptoed into Blossom's bed room and placed it on the foot of her bed. Marcy phoned in the morning, but Blossom was still fast asleep, so she phoned her back again that evening, she had phoned Blossom to see how she was feeling and to say everyone was missing her in school March Twenty-Three, finally for the first time in what to Blossom seemed to be for ever, she was able to go back to school to all her friends. Blossom was still a little weak from the flu, but she was over it. When Blossom had arrived home that afternoon, there was a magazine waiting for her at the front door, "Three weeks before to that date she had cancelled out the magazine. March Twenty-Four, Well today the school recorded every one's height and weight, Blossom was always shy to show her weight to anyone, but they did manage to talk her into getting her weight recorded in the nurse's office. She was five foot six and three quarters, her weight she didn't write in her diary. March Twenty-Six, Saturday the Cartwright's and the William's all went out to a beautiful park with the kids. They had dinner at a drive-in restaurant, you can eat in your car, they will slide a tray through the window; that fastened on each side of the car windows, Casey's treat.

March Twenty-Eight, was asked to work in the school office, running off test papers; on the duplicating machine, Blossom really enjoyed it, she got home very tired and did the dinner dishes, then went straight to bed.

April One, April fool day, phoned Carol in the morning and played an April fools joke on her. Then watched the "Magnificent seven "movie; went to bed after the movie. Casey played a good April fools joke on Blossom, she would fall for it every time, since she loved horses so much. April Two, Cynthia, Willette and Blossom all went shopping, bought a pretty blouse, white and blue in color with ruffled lace down the front, Blossom also had bought shoulder length bag and a full length white slip, she then met Norman.

The very next day Carol had phoned her again, Hal's family, Patrick and Diana came over. Blossom had just skinned her left knee before they had arrived, so she wasn't feeling well. She went straight into bed. Blossom didn't like the sight of Blood, it made her woozy. April Fifth, Nineteen Sixty-Six, This was the fourth night of the full moon, that full moon reminded her so much of when she first met Larry, she had just baked a white layer cake that evening and then fell asleep on the love seat in the living room, when Larry had come over to borrow a cup of sugar, he noticed her lying there, looking so innocent as he would say."

April Six, Casey put two hundred and fifty dollars in each of the four daughters' accounts that day. Mrs. Dorothy called Blossom out of the classroom that morning to work in the school office. Blossom was also given a rubbing alcohol for rash of pimples, all over her face. The following day not too much happened. April Eighth, Good Friday, Hal's family and all the Cartwright's except Cynthia, were out helping Dawn in her strawberry field weeding. Blossom made five dollars and sixty cents. Dawn always paid for the help with the strawberry field even if it was family, she had four acres Easter Sunday Blossom was first one up to go to Church. She genuinely enjoyed going to church services, it was the church in town which also was the first day that the Cartwright's didn't have any company. April Eleventh, Blossom received in the mail an answer to the art contest she had sent out a month ago. The art contest was to see how well you could draw; it was a lumber Jack's face you had to draw free handed out of the news paper.

April Twelfth, Tuesday Cynthia and Blossom went shopping at dollar forty nine day, (dollar forty nine day was when you can buy most things for one dollar and forty nine cents), came home and watched the show called Paten Place, did some drawing for the contest next to come. Blossom still was having those seizures, but they weren't as bad as before. On April Fourteen, she did some more art pictures; Cynthia, and Blossom watched the Thursday night movies together. In those days Cynthia, and Blossom were getting along a little better. "Maybe someday they will get along and be good friends, "thought Dawn."

April Fifteen, Took a picture of Willette in her new outfit, then watched the "Wild West show, two men came over to see Dawn, but she didn't know what they wanted just then.

April Seventeenth, Nineteen Sixty-Six, Willette wasn't feeling too well that day. Carol phoned again, then we watched combat on TV, helped pick more weeds from Dawn's strawberry field. It didn't seem like there was much to do those days. Carol was a girl from school that Blossom chummed around with. She turned out to be a bit of a tramp after, so Blossom stopped seeing her and stayed friends with Lana. April Eighteen, Everyone at school liked the new blouse Blossom had bought on dollar forty nine day." The two men came back to see Dawn. Casey went to see them this time too. They turned out to be insurance men trying to sell Dawn life insurance. Blossom worked hard all day in the school office again. April Nineteen, have you ever felt lonely in your own home? "Well I do writes Blossom, she said when she gets out into the working world, she no longer feels lonely," because she feels wanted and loved, she had been feeling pretty low that day. Some days she would say to herself that she wished she lived in a home not just a fancy house April Twenty, there was a boy sent to the office in the afternoon for being caught with a bottle of perfume, to make a long story short, the principal gave the perfume to Blossom to keep. The next day Carol and Blossom went to a movie in town, and then Carol stayed for dinner and spent the night with Blossom. Blossom's diary then skipped to April Twenty-Fourth, on which Carol and Blossom took some film back down to be processed, Carol stayed for dinner and the night again. The girls were at the age where they'd lay awake talking about boys all night long. The next day they did a lot of walking up and down the long steep hill to and from town. April Twenty-Fifth, Blossom curled her hair and watched the "Big Valley" a movie in the afternoon. Uncle Dudley and Aunty Vera came over after dinner for a short visit then left again. Blossom says, "Different times Sheila and Cynthia use to try and snoop into her diary which was on the head board of her bed, in her room behind closed doors. Blossom would have her most precious thoughts written down on those papers, "then she would catch them snickering and laughing about it later to themselves. So one day she wrote something very interesting, but juicy in her diary just to assist their curiosity, only they didn't know that Blossom had made it all up, it was all about sex.

April Twenty-Six, Wednesday worked in the school office again, Della phoned, she's now working in a hospital on Johnston road. Della was another one of Blossom's school friends, she is doing laundry there.

April Twenty-Seven, Jr. high school had their concert, Blossom was suppose to be in the choir, but she didn't go instead she worked in the school office again loving every minute of it.

April Twenty-Eight, Blossom hadn't kept her diary up for one whole year now, what ever happened in that year of her life no one knows. However she did mention then she had gone to the municipal hall for an application form, then she sat down and wrote her sister Sheila a letter. Blossom liked to write to Sheila and receive letters back.

April Twenty-Nine, Nineteen Sixty-Seven, Blossom went on to say, last year around the same time at eight-thirty PM they had an earth quake. The large evergreen tree just out side the window of Blossom and Cynthia's bedroom, fell along the side of their house that evening, it managed not to destroy anything in the process. Blossom writes in her diary on April Thirty, that you can please some of the people some of the time, but you can't please all the people all of the time. That was such a true description, why she had written that in her diary she couldn't remember. Anyway Blossom would go on with her Story; the earth quake rattled some of the people's houses that evening.

May fifth, Dear Diary, "there was another full moon to night, didn't do too much though," just baked a chocolate cake and worked in the flower garden out front; until it had gotten too late to do any more weeding, my rose bushes are really beautiful now, with large pink blooms.

May Sixth, Blossom was worried sick about her parents, Blossom had gotten home from school late that afternoon, the doors were all locked and her parents weren't home, they had never in the past gone out without leaving some kind of a note for the girls first. Casey and Dawn had gotten home around seven that evening, Blossom was fast asleep waiting up for them on the couch.

May Seven, Well Carol, Lana and Blossom all went roller skating, Blossom was getting pretty good on her roller skates. After they all went to the nursery for a pink rose bush, which was called "PINK PRINCESS."

May eighth, Mother's day, Sunday, Dawn had received a beautiful rhododendron plant, from Casey. Blossom had finished planting everything in her garden out front. It was a piece of land along the fence line about five feet by three feet, Each for Blossom and Cynthia for their very own garden.

May ninth, Monday everything went wrong today, had more seizures and to top it all off Dawn didn't believe it when she told her about her seizures. She practically called Blossom a liar. That made Blossom upset and have even more seizures. She thinks that her mother just doesn't want to admit that there was something wrong with their Blossom.

May Tenth, Dear Diary, "After school I had gone out to help mom in the back field; picking roots and rocks, some of those rock were really heavy to lift. Lana stayed for dinner; again. May Eleventh, "Am writing this in the morning," says Blossom," because if I ever have a little girl or boy that I would call them Betty Jean and Darcy Donald." May the Twelve, Blossom was still writing in her book that she had hoped one day she would be able to get her book published, she worked again in the school office that afternoon keeping very busy.

May Thirteenth, Friday; eleven o'clock AM, "went to watch the movie, "TICKLE" with Carol and Lana. The following day Dawn got her planter, Blossom watched a little TV, Wrote some more in her book called, 'A COUNTRY CITY LOVE.'

May seventeenth, phone Carol, being a Sunday the family didn't go to church though, this time instead Blossom wrote some stories in her book. She could only write when ever there was no one else around to bug her, since her sisters use to make fun of her ideas on paper, and the fact that she believed that some day she was going to get her book published, but little did they know, that with all that fun making of her ideas, someday she was determined to get her book published, it just made her all the more determined to go though with it. I guess she had to show them that she could accomplish something. The next day they went to school as usual and then the Theater.

May Eighteenth, Blossom's relatives came over and she made 88 cents picking rocks from the strawberry field. After the Fenton's came back from the funeral, they were invited over for dinner at the Cartwright's, so Aunty Mae wouldn't have to do any cooking that evening, Dawn was always thoughtful in that way.

May Nineteenth, Dawn, Casey and Willette; went to uncle Fenton's. The following day Carol and Blossom had fun at the local fair with Lana, Blossom made $2.90 painting the long fence, along the side of their property it was painted white for Casey. This took place in the late afternoon, that evening they all went to Seattle to spend the night and shop.

May Twenty-One, Dear Diary, "It's raining again today in Seattle, got up around seven or seven-thirty," I can't remember just exactly which time it was, anyway we were to get ready to leave for home today. "I had bought myself the night before a pretty shell sweater, in a real nice white with little pink flowers on the yolk.

May Twenty-Two, played the recorder with Elvis Presley record that was bought in the States on our holidays, it was called "GIRL HAPPY"

May Twenty-Fourth, Dear Diary, "didn't bother to write yesterday, had a lot of seizures again, I sure wish they would go away and never come back. After school; went to see the Optometrist with dad. "Was not much more that was interesting."

May Twenty-Fifth, "Got a letter from the Williams; they write that the senior Williams are coming up to visit them this summer; Oh! I didn't tell you they are back together now, have been for some time since the wedding.

May Twenty-Six, "Went to the Rodeo with some girl friends, we all had a riot on the rides. "Arrived home around six o'clock PM, "just in time to make dinner.

May Twenty-Seventh, "Had a appointment at the optometrist Again at two in the afternoon, "Dad drove me there and back since it was way across town. In the evening we all went to a movie and saw "SONS OF KATE ADEN'.

May Twenty-Eighth, "Went to bed at twenty-five to two AM, was up again at nine A.M. departed out of the house for Uncle Jed's cabin on the lake at twelve-thirty.

May Thirty," Stayed home in the morning with Cynthia and Willette, took Rusty, our golden Labrador dog for a walk. Different times he almost got away from her. The next day Blossom says that age makes no difference when you are in Love, she thinks that she is in Love with Larry.

Chapter Five

The Summer Months.

The following month being the first day of June, Blossom and her dad wrote a letter to the William's family. Casey put his letter in with Blossom's to save on stamps, Blossom had being thinking of doing some private typing for a career, she really like doing typing, that was her passion. Her parents had been discussing the fact about building a joining office next to Casey's in the basement, then hiring Blossom to work for him. She also had been trying out a few recipes from the collection of recipes she clipped out of the news paper, some of them were: Peanut Butter and Fudge, the fancy fudge recipe was the one her family just loved her to make the most. On the following day Blossom had an IQ test at school, she past it with flying colors, also the typewriter that her mom had ordered came in on Monday the following week. This being a Friday, Willette and Cynthia went for their piano lessons, which was just around the corner from the school. Their lessons lasted from four PM. to six PM.; Willette was learning modern music Cynthia was learning classical. Blossom had wished that her mother would let her take music lessons too, but Dawn was afraid of her having a seizure while she was away from her. Blossom was reminiscing about nineteen sixty-six the same time the school had given out P.N.E. tickets to all the children in the school, in order to get into the grounds free but being that Blossom was sick at home that day she missed out on one. June the fourth was the day she had bought Casey a father's day gift, Blossom had picked out a beautiful pair of black Alaska diamond cuff links with silver links; they were the perfect pair for her dad Blossom thought to herself.

Sunday, the following day, everyone went to church in the morning. Then after church the Cartwright's had a lot of friends over. Some of them brought their little poodle dog, others stayed for dinner, Eldon and Grace Mathews, Brenda and Otto Brown, Hal's family of six, Ross and Sybil Dole and the minister and his wife with their two children.

Monday when the typewriter came in, Dawn wasn't pleased with the typewriter at all; she had received it late that afternoon to start with, which ruined her whole day for planning anything. When she had opened the box, it was the wrong typewriter she ordered; the very next day she exchanged it for another electric typewriter in the color of beige and olive green. Dawn's Idea was that Cynthia and Blossom could take turns using the electrical typewriter for their school studies.

This was now June the eighth, last year around the same time Blossom remembers as she rocked back and forth in her rocking chair, "she had her braces that straightened her two upper teeth, taken off, her two front teeth use to push all the way in and the tooth on each side of the those teeth use to stick way out, but Blossom still had to wear a mouth piece when ever she had gone to bed, the mouth piece was a tiny thin wire that was hooked onto the silver metal piece mounted in her mouth. Blossom's mouth was full of silver metal thin wires that had been put on her teeth to straightened them, by using the mouth piece it put pressure in the mouth; on the teeth that helped to straighten them, there was a padded piece that went around the back of her head; then the other side of the tiny thin wire that was attached to the left inside of the mouth on the metal. In nineteen sixty-seven again, Blossom was still wearing that same mouth piece, but sometimes she would forget to wear it at night, Blossom just refused to open her mouth as long as she still had those horrible metal piece in her mouth. "The mouth piece was about six inches long and curved in the middle to the shape of the face on the outside of her mouth." It was easy enough to undo, in order to take it off, when she eats.

By now Betty was turning one year old, on June ninth, she had a wonderful birthday party with balloons and presents at her Grandmother Cartwright's home, Blossom had caught another bad cold that day.

The very next day; the entire Cartwright family had picked strawberries to put on the market, from Dawn's field; which was four acres by now. Dawn would sell the berries that day and pay the pickers each week for their services. Most of the pickers were either family or relatives trying to earn a little extra money for the summer months ahead. On June the eleventh Saturday, Blossom had picked nine carriers of strawberries in the heat of the day. The following day she picked more strawberries and wrote more pages in her book. By this time Blossom was on her third chapter in the book she was writing called "COUNTRY CITY LOVE." When Dawn had asked Blossom if she would rather stay home and pick strawberries in the field, she agreed, but Blossom really wanted to go to school. By the time that Monday had rolled around she had changed her mind and went to school. Blossom wanted to make something more out of her self, even though she still had the seizures. Blossom still went off to school to learn how to become a good writer someday. She always was eager to learn new ideas.

June Fourteen, Blossom stayed away from school, since her cold was getting worse instead of better, but she refused to stay in bed all day while her mother was slaving away out side in the heat, picking strawberries by herself. So Blossom worked like a horse along side her mother picking strawberries for Dawn, Dawn would insist on paying her for her help.

When Saturday came, they were back out there picking all the berries they could before the summer rain came. Cynthia and Dawn were busy grading them in the field shed that Casey built for Dawn earlier in the year, while the rest of the family were out in the field picking berries in the hot sun Picking those berries was really hard to do that day, since it was so hot and sticky in the afternoon. Blossom would say," you had to really watch you didn't get a sun stroke or if you drank too much cold water too fast at once you would end up with stomach cramps. That evening there was thunder showers, which didn't last too long, they all stopped for a short while picking; then went back at it again after the showers stopped. On the following Monday Blossom didn't go to school; instead she stayed home to help her mother again pick those darn berries before they rotted on the vine from the thunder showers.

Tuesday, Roy and Henry each made two dollars and thirty-five cents picking strawberries in the last hour. Blossom herself made five dollars in the last couple of hours to bring her earnings up to thirty dollars; she would pick over 200 carriers of strawberries in the last week. To Blossom that was a lot of money.

Then came Father's day, Blossom was able to save enough money to pay off her bill on the black Alaska diamond cuff links for her dad, she gave them to Casey in the morning before he had a chance to disappear into his work shop; just out side in the garage, Blossom also gave him a big kiss and Father's day card that she had made herself.

Willette and Dawn gave Casey a card to say that his Father's day gift was still coming. Again Blossom was reminiscing, in the last year at around the same time of the year in which they had to pick rocks and roots to get the field ready for planting strawberry plants, by machine. It looked something like a tractor, only at the bottom the plants came out and someone else would go walking behind, usually it was Casey behind the machine to be sure that the plants were firmly planted in the ground. There were some fairly large rocks and roots that had to come up, and then put out on the home-made stone boat that was pulled behind the field tractor, sometimes Blossom was aloud to drive the tractor, she enjoyed that very much.

After all the roots and rocks were picked up and dragged off with the stone boat, then they were put in a neat pile, that's when they would start cultivating on the hard ground, then and only then the machine would come along and plant the strawberry plants. When that was all done, they would have to irrigate the field and spray for insects etc. Blossom made ninety dollars working in the field that summer. The following day had a real sing song going in the smaller field while still picking the berries in the heat of the day, Blossom just had to stop writing in her book to listen to them. On Friday, a very hot day again, Blossom started picking strawberries for her mother, but before her day had ended she had decided to quit early so she could help in the selling end of the berries down on the busy highway. Her parents had a strawberry stand out on the highway; that Casey had built for her a few weeks prior. That highway was a very busy one, with all the cars going by; to go into town, it was a good place for setting up to sell strawberries, In the evening the sunset was like a ball of fire ever so pretty.

When Blossom had worked the next morning, she had to watch that she wasn't going to get too much sun in the heat of the day, this way she could control her seizures some what, Blossom's quite fair so she would also get headaches, sometimes quite bad ones from the sun. The next morning Aunt Mae came over to help out in the berry field; Blossom stayed in the house and watched TV. Just took it rather easy in the house; as not to get her seizures starting up again. She watched a show called "WILD IN THE COUNTRY," staring Elvis Presley, She really liked his shows were the best. Blossom didn't write in her book too much that day, however she writes on the following day another chapter.

As Blossom leaned back in her rocker; she said in those days she was still thinking about Larry, in those few days she had thought a lot more of him than ever before. Blossom only picked a carrier of strawberries that morning, but in the afternoon she washed the kitchen floor and made lunch for everyone, then Sheila phoned long distance.

On the Twenty-ninth of June was only a half day of school for everyone, the teachers had a meeting in the afternoon, Carol's little dog had pups, two male and three females, only two females and one male pup lived through the birth. Carol said they all had thought that her dog was spayed.

Blossom's seizures are not too bad these days. She had hoped that this year she would get a typing job, since she was practicing all summer on Dawn's typewriter and loved every minute of it. The only thing Blossom didn't count on, was how that people with Epilepsy would have such a hard time in getting any kind of a job, because the public in general, mostly the business people in the working world in those days, and some in these days too thinks that anyone with a psychological problem such as epilepsy; or a lighter case being Petit-Mal, as in Blossom's case are some kind of freaks, the way that they put it, is that it is too much of a accident risk, that was a bunch of bull, As Blossom was saying this you could see it in her face that she was reliving the whole episode, the humiliation she had been put through back then, then she would say with a rough tone to her voice, "people with epilepsy are no more an accident risk than any normal person is. The problem with the business man or woman in those days are, that they just don't know enough about epilepsy, and didn't want to learn about it either, so they pass judgment unfairly on those who have epilepsy. On the following day the family allowance cheque came in. Dawn always gave them over to the girls for their clothing, as they were old enough now to pick out their own clothing. So then after picking berries all day, Blossom's cheque came in the mail, she had her eye on a very pretty baby blue cotton dress, with frills down the front. At the end of the day Dawn treated everyone out at the Dairy Queen for a milk shake; in the old blue pick-up truck. Casey drove.

By the first of July, it had rained all day and quite heavy too, might I add, but they still had to pick those strawberries before they would rot out in the field and Dawn would loose all that money sitting in the field

July Second, the Cartwright's all went to see a movie in the new theater down town, got home fairly late that evening, then just went straight to bed, since their legs just wouldn't carry them any further, the whole family was so tired from working out in the heavy rain; in the berry field earlier that day.

The next morning the old cherry tree out front was full with cherries and ready to be picked, Hal's family of six came over that afternoon to help out in the picking of the strawberries, then Casey and Blossom picked a couple of buckets of cherries for Hal's family to take home. These cherries were a little extra for helping with the strawberries earlier. Dawn would always give them a bucket or two of cherries to take home with them, they were the Bing cherries, the good tasting ones, Then Blossom writes more in her book again that day. Then came the fourth day of July, Uncle Fenton's family went to a wedding in Saskatchewan, they left in the morning and the Cartwright's had offered to look after their dog, a Collie pup, Cartwright's had given the children a year ago for Christmas.

By the time the fifth of July rolled around it was still raining practically all day again, Dawn took Blossom out to get her hair cut shorter, and after dinner the whole family had helped with the dishes. The girls all went shopping again.

Wednesday, some of Blossom's relatives came over about five thirty from the fruit valley and stayed the night. The next day they left for the Islands. On the seventh of July some more relatives came from the prairies and stayed the night at the Cartwright's home again. Then they went to find a place to live out West in the Valley. Blossom picked more berries the following day and the day after that too, she picked in the morning five carriers and one in the afternoon, being a Saturday they all went out for dinner at the A & W Restaurant.

By the time the eleventh of July rolled around, the Cartwright's were still looking after the collie pup, Casey was now in the hospital with kidney stones. A year ago that summer Dawn and Casey had bought a new car and everyone had a ride in it. The following morning after Dawn got up and dressed, she had taken all the girls out on a shopping spree, Dawn left the girls shopping, while she had gone up to the hospital to see Casey.

On the next day Blossom had got paid from work, then Dawn and Uncle Jed both went up to see Casey in the hospital, after their short visit was finished and they came back home, they talked for a little while before they took everyone out for a milk shake. Then the next day; Casey phoned at noon from the hospital corridors to say that he was being released tomorrow. It was eleven o'clock the next day now. In nineteen sixty-five; Blossom was getting ready for the very first time, she had never flown in a airplane, it was around the same time of the year as the blossoms were just coming out in bloom, that was how she had remembered it so well. That was a year in which she would never forget, July fifteen nineteen sixty-five." Boy! It sure was good to have dad home again," Blossom would say, getting back to the present year again. Then on Sunday everyone went first to church to give thanks and then after church the whole family all drove over to see Hal's family, Hal's family were back home now and they had a lot to talk about, and lots of laughs that afternoon too. By ten o'clock the next morning they just came out of the dentist office from a check up with the girls. As soon as Blossom got home she sat down at her desk and finished her book. The Cartwright's all went out again for dinner and a milk shake, the treat Dawn had promised them for later, while they were out they met some old friends of the family, Roger and Diana Bates. The following day; Wednesday being, the Cartwright's had finished their weeding and all went shopping down at the new shopping center, it had just opened up. In those days they did a lot of shopping, "Blossom would go on to say." While shopping they had met some more friends of the family from years ago, these people use to be their neighbors, so the Cartwright's invited them over for a cup of coffee. Blossom was only four years old when the Cartwright's had moved away from the old neighborhood, but she still remembered them. The following morning she went out weeding again in her flower garden, then at ten to twelve she came in and made lunch for everyone. That evening she had finished fertilizing and watering her flower garden, then went to bed early. Next morning when Blossom had awoken her uncle Fenton's family was back, they came to pick up Lassie, Boy! were those kids ever glad to see her. Two days later Blossom was back at the dentist, which was about all that had happened in the morning. By the afternoon she was outside weeding again, came in at eight PM. for the evening. July thirteen, a friend named Dolly came over, around four and showed Blossom her engagement ring, it was a tiny white gold band with three little diamonds in a cluster on top. At that point in time she had asked Blossom to be her bridesmaid. Blossom had more seizures that day, since she had let herself get too excited, about Dolly's wedding, since she never got to be Sheila's bridesmaid. Blossom had quite a time picking all those berries and making enough money to go on a holiday. In those summer months, Blossom's seizures were getting fewer and fewer each day she had been waiting for the day that her prayers would be answered and she would no longer have to watch herself from having those seizures any more.

Chapter Six

Blossom's First Hope Chest

In the year nineteen sixty-seven, Casey gave Blossom her first hope chest, it use to belong to her grandmother Cartwright, which consisted of a large old heavy type travel trunk, black in color with a brown leather type belt wrapped around the middle to hold the lid on. Blossom then bought some blue flowered wall paper and redid the entire inside; Casey was in the middle of building a shelf that would sit just inside the trunk, then Blossom would wall paper that shelf to match the rest.

On August first Casey and Dawn gave Blossom her very first piece to go in her hope chest, it was a beautiful seven piece crystal set, consisted of cream and sugar bowl, butter dish with lid and salt and pepper That set was originally bought for a workman daughter's wedding, they were suppose to go to, but didn't. Instead Blossom was given it for her hope chest. In time to come Blossom would buy a two hundred dollar Royal Albert china dinner set of eight for her hope chest. She had saved a little money out of each pay cheques towards the dinner set, she had seen it earlier in the hardware store and her heart was set on getting that particular dinner set for a very long time.

The second day of August, Blossom did more weeding in her flower garden, then she helped finish the weeding in the berry field that afternoon. She washed the den floor for her mother, and then they started to get ready for the holidays. The Cartwright's had been planning a trip to Kalowna to their Aunt Lola's for some time now, by ten PM. on the fifth of August the Cartwright's family arrived in Kalowna on Aunty Lolo's door step.

Saturday, a hot sunny day, the two families went out shopping at the new Kalowna center, then took the girls out to the zoo, Blossom use to enjoy going to the zoo to see all those animals. The Cartwright family stayed until August eight, right after breakfast they left for their long trip home. They had arrived home eight P.M. the next day; Casey had to start back to work, so they all went to bed early.

On that Monday afternoon, the first day of the beginning of a work week, Blossom got some very disappointing news, the boy Larry that she had fallen in love with, had another girl friend, she was very good looking, thought Blossom, She lived in Clover green Meadows. Well Blossom just took that day very easy for fear that she might have another seizure.

On the following day she had gone over to the neighbors with Willette and Sheila, while they were over picking apples, some old friends of her parents dropped into see them. Mr. and Mrs. Woodley, when the girls came back home they gave them some of the freshly picked apples to take home with them, the girls were always taught to be generous. August the eleventh, the country fair was going on, and being too hot, much too hot to do work outside, the Cartwright's home wasn't too far from the fair grounds, Blossom and her sisters all went in the afternoon across the open field where they got in free. The girls had to crawl under a barb wire fence to get into the country fair so they would sneak in. In the evening Casey took them again, only this time he paid their way in, Dawn wanted to stay home and spray her strawberry plants, so dad just took his three Daughters, they had a wail of a good time. The Cartwright's left for Port Hardy, three days after they had a wail of a time at the country fair, were all in good spirits, They left their golden lab, Rusty with Fenton's family this time.

The sixteenth of August Blossom was just finishing up doing the dishes in the small trailer at the park side, her parents had bought her a little Baleena camera, they had all ready seen the Buchard gardens; in Victoria and had lots of pictures of them. Next day they went fishing, Blossom took many pictures of them catching their dinner, she use to enjoy going fishing with her dad, even though Casey didn't go too often. While they were still at the campsite in Port Hardy, they decided to visit Sheila's family who wasn't too far away from where they had been camped.

By now the twenty-third of August had rolled around, the Cartwright's had arrived back home, they picked up Rusty, Was! Blossom ever so glad to see her dog again, she began combing him out until his coat shinned, then they all went out shopping for some new clothes, for school that started next month. Up to this point in the book it probably sounds like your ever day person, but remember Blossom was fighting epilepsy that she had to deal with day by day. If you read on it will get a lot better believe me.

Back to the story, Cynthia never did anything like washing a dog down, she use to say, "that wasn't lady like," but Blossom figured that someone had to do it, and better than a fight starting she would end up being the one to do it anyway.

On Thursday Blossom had realized that the puppy love she had for Larry was just a faze she had gone through. While Blossom was telling this story about her life, she remembered the time she had flown to the Charlottes by her self. She'd taken off to visit her sister Sheila and family, Betty was just a baby then. Blossom would enjoy watching the two children for Sheila, if she had to go any place. Blossom was always over whelmed to be able to be trusted to watch the kids for her.

One day Grant, who worked for the airlines company had asked Blossom if she would like to take a ride in a airplane with some of the other guys, they would be delivering the goods to the logging camps along the riverside. Blossom just jumped for the chance to go, it was a little water plane that only seated six passengers, Blossom was the only girl in the plane, the other five seats were filled with men that worked on the ground crew. They all let Blossom sit up front in the co-pilots seat. The pilot was a half breed and a very nice person too, he showed Blossom what the different instruments were used for, then at one point in the demonstration he even asked Blossom if she would like to fly the plane, but Blossom had decided not to even though, she would of loved flying, but she was afraid that she might have a seizure and crash the plane then someone would be badly hurt. Blossom didn't tell him it was because of her epilepsy, she just declined gracefully. Deep down inside her feelings she was wishing she never had those darn seizures, because they were keeping her away from so many ventures she would like to be able to do in her life time, flying a plane was one of Blossom's dreams. She also knew she would never have another chance to fly a plane. She was a little shy and this time she was even a little afraid of being the only girl in the plane, but she had known that her brother-n-law Grant wouldn't let anything happen to her, she trusted Grant. The name of the little plane was the Beaver, the little Island hops. If anyone wanted a ride back to the Island, then Blossom would of been bumped off the plane, that meant that since she was travailing for free she would have to get off, the pilot would then have to come back for her later, Fortunately Blossom wasn't bumped off. In the boxes at the back of the plane was food and clothing for the winter; as well as tools for the loggers. We had flown to three different camp sites all together, while still in the day light, it rained, hailed, snowed, and then the sun came out, but not before the fog had rolled in, this all happened before they had landed the plane back at the airport. Finally a rainbow came, by the time the plane had landed. Blossom was as white as a ghost and feeling rather faint, but she never fainted. The next day it rained all day like cats and dogs, again Blossom helped with the children changing and then later helped in making supper, Later that evening Sheila took Blossom out shopping while Grant baby sat. That was way back in Nineteen sixty-five and now it was nineteen sixty-seven. August twenty-eight a Sunday, the Cartwright's all went to church.

The day before she was with her family down at Uncle Jed's home on the lake again, they went boating, swimming and just goofing around.

That was something Blossom really liked to do was to swim, but if no one else was around by the lake then she wasn't aloud to go in swimming, incase she had a seizure and drowned. Dawn worried about her a lot. Dawn was afraid that her seizures would come while she was alone swimming and Blossom might drown without anyone knowing where she was. When they all finished swimming or boating they would have a game Badminton out back with all the adults, usually it was the adults against the children including nieces and nephews, there was always more children than adults in the game.

By the time they had arrived home the next day, Dawn was very happy she had lost 3 pounds that week. One of the neighbor's boy; named Allen came over and then they all went out to the Pacific National Exhibition in the evening. She didn't have any seizures that day.

On August the twenty-ninth that Casey had taken them all down to the Army and Navy department store to do some school shopping and being so generous he then treated everyone out for a milk shake at the Dairy Queen, Casey loved milk shakes.

Earlier in the day Casey took Willette and Blossom out to an auction sale, after they all went to a man's home where they looked at some sheep. Blossom didn't know his name, Casey had just met him at the auction, he wanted to see about buying some ewes, Blossom was still working on the finishing touches of her book, and that day she finally finished the entire story after three long years of retyping it, just so no spelling mistakes would appear in it. She was still hoping that some day she would get her book published, of course the rest of the family thought that it was really ridiculous to even think that there might be even a little chance that her book could possibly be published.

On September sixteen Blossom went potato picking, she made thirteen dollars picking and digging potatoes up by hand, out in the field, there was no machine that did the work like now a days, it rained in the morning sometimes, but mostly in the morning it was very foggy, then one day in the afternoon some of the owner's cow would get out of the next pasture, and start running through the entire potato field, where all the pickers were down on their hands and knees just as busy as could be, picking and digging the potatoes, putting them into buckets and then into potato sacks. The bags were made of gunny sack materials, tying the bags up with twine to be ready for transport on the old wooden truck. The pickers had to keep a record of the sacks they picked each day in order to be paid the proper wages. Next day Blossom didn't have a partner, you see everyone was to have a partner to make it easier for dumping into the sacks. Well that day she did it all by herself and she picked seventy-two and half sacks full.

Dawn would pick Blossom up around four-thirty every evening, she would drive into the long winding driveway and wait for Blossom there, Blossom had just hopped off the back of the old wooden truck, were they had piled the potato sacks to haul up to the barn. When she had arrived home she was so dirty and tired that she just jumped into a hot soapy tub and soaked for an hour or so.

After that she came down stairs to the kitchen for dinner that was still waiting in the oven for her, did up the supper dishes for her mother. By the time eight o'clock came around she was up stairs fast asleep in her double bed.

Next evening Dawn, Blossom and an old friend of the family's took a course at night school. Dawn and Sally had signed up for a typing class, but didn't get too much typing done. Blossom however took up creative writing and enjoyed ever minute of it. She had to do some homework of creative writing about Tokyo.

When October the second rolled around, Blossom had planted most of her flowers in the front flower garden, came in washed up and made pop corn. Casey decided to take a trip down to a riding academy with Blossom and Cynthia to look for a horse for Blossom. Since Blossom had been asking, or should I say begging for a horse of her own for the last thirteen years. The last three weeks Blossom had started making long distance phone calls in order to buy a horse. At that point in time Casey and Dawn both decided that maybe a horse would be cheaper than to have to pay all those long distance phone calls, Blossom was making. Blossom was still looking for a typing job at that time, she figured she had found the right job, then would try and win two-thousand dollars in a puzzle; that was in one of the magazine, she found while skimming through it one afternoon. In time to come though Blossom would discover that she would not hear back from those people ever again.

October sixth, Blossom had phoned three different people about a horse for sale. They were all thorough bred horses, you know the more expensive ones, which back in those days five hundred dollars was expensive for a horse, the phone calls ended up costing more than what Dawn and Casey could afford at the time. When Casey, Blossom and Cynthia went out looking for a horse, they found the right one for Blossom, Casey wanted a gentle horse for his girls, Blossom wanted one that was spirited enough to teach to jump or barrel race someday, she had high expatiations.

The very first place they had gone to, the horse was costing over three hundred dollars and the second place there was two horses for sale, both were too high in price, one was a champion race horse, the third place they called on also had caught Blossom's eye in the paper, read: "WITH SADDLE AND BRIDLE ONLY THREE HUNDRED DOLLARS, but Casey and Dawn decided that a race horse would be too spirited for their daughters. The Cartwright's were thinking that if Blossom has one of her seizures while riding, what! would happen to Blossom then. Blossom wasn't sleeping too well in those days. She just had too more pages to rewrite in her chapter and didn't know exactly how she was going to end the chapter.

Blossom had been expanding her hope chest that day, she had quite a few pieces of china, even some under her bed, this double bed use to belong to her parents before they had bought twin beds.

Blossom remembers, "One night," a long time ago; on a October black night, the eleventh it was, "she said her father hit her several times with an army belt until she just felt like turning over and dying. Blossom had figured that it was because she was talking to Cynthia;, instead of going to sleep, who she shared the same bedroom, but she wasn't sure, because Cynthia never got a beating and she was talking too. Blossom goes on to say, "that usually it had something to do with Cynthia, as Cynthia always found some way to get her into trouble. When Blossom tried to defend herself they just closed their ears and eyes to her.

On October thirteen it was Blossom's fourth night at the creative class; at night school. Last night she had more seizures than usual at her class, for awhile Blossom thought that she had been getting over them, it was Blossom's greatest wish to be able to have that kind of a career in writing.

September thirteen rolled around the following year, it was Blossom's thirteenth birthday. In the mail that day came a belated birthday gift from the William's, a box filled with under clothing and a couple pairs of nylon stockings, "I guess Sheila thought that the box wouldn't arrive on time to Blossom, and that was why she had written; belated on the card. Dawn, Cynthia and Willette gave Blossom a tweed skirt and matching blouse, that Dawn had made herself. Casey's name was usually added to the gifts and cards, some of the time he didn't even know what he was giving them.

The next night being a Saturday she stayed up until eleven o'clock watching a movie called, "BYE BYE BIRDIE."

Next morning still being very hot out, the Cartwright's held a welcome to B.C. party, in their newly finished rec-room, which was in the coolness of the basement. Dawn's old school friend had moved with her family into a new home, a small place out on the crest, the party lasted until quarter pasted one in the morning.

Blossom tried using yeast in those days, an old remedy to get rid of pimples, now a days they call them zits, she had a lot of those nasty pimples all over her face, unfortunately the yeast wasn't working either.

Well Blossom was getting tired of always being turned down with her typing applications, she was so determined to get a job, she then decided to apply at the new Bay department store as a clerk, Cynthia had gotten a job there the other day and they were still hiring, but Blossom had gotten turned down on that one too, because of her schooling she figures, she hated that special school, it has followed her all through life and it seemed to be a curse on her. Then in the next week and being a Saturday, it was Dawn's and Casey's anniversary, their twenty-fifth to be exact. Cynthia's birthday landed on the day before, so they always celebrated together with Cynthia, they had planned on meeting some friends and all going out to dinner together. The friends they were meeting were actually Casey's kissing cousins, a family joke between cousins, their family and the Cartwright's. They all had it planned that when Casey and Dawn had arrived at their home they would all transfer over into the cousin's car. As soon as the three of them had left the house, Willette and Blossom quickly sneaked out the back door, after hurrying up and getting dressed into their good clothes, then went straight out to the Forest Century to meet the Grover's who Dawn and Casey had given the welcome to B.C. party to earlier. From there the Grover's took the girls over to their home, in which the Cartwright's (girls) and the Grover's had planned a twenty-fifth anniversary party. As a surprise for them, the party theme was of Hawaii, since Dawn and Casey always wanted to go to Hawaii, but never could afford it. Well! when Dawn had stepped into the house and went down stairs where the party was being held, she saw Willette and Blossom straight ahead standing in front of her, at that point seeing the two girls standing there, when she had thought they were still at home, Dawn went into a daze, A matter of a fact before coming into the house Dawn had thought something was up and had said to Casey, Oh no we left the girls at home." She thought that the girls were going to miss out on a fun party. At that time little did she know that right inside that door stood Willette and Blossom as proud as punch to be there? It was a very big surprise with the three girls standing in front, wearing leis around their necks to present to their parents. Everyone had chipped in one dollar to which they exchanged for a silver dollar that was placed on the home made money tree. That was a lot of fun that evening, the following week in the local news paper an ad read:

"AN HAWAII THEME WAS THE SETTING FOR A SURPRISE GATHERING AT THEIR FRIENDS AND RELATIVES IN HONOR OF THEIR SILVER ANNIVERSARY ON OCTOBER TWENTY-SECOND FOR DAWN AND CASEY CARTWRIGHT.

HAVING HAD TO CANCEL THEIR PLANS OF FLYING TO HAWAII FOR THE OCCASION MR. AND MRS. GROVER OF VANCOUVER AND MR. AND MRS. DUDDLEY OF BURNABY STREET, LIFE LONG FRIENDS OF THE CARTWRIGHT'S DECIDED TO BRING HAWAII TO THEM. MR. AND MRS. GROVER HOSTED THE SURPRISE PARTY AT THEIR LOVELY HOME. WITH A LOT OF HELP IN THE ORGANIZING BY MR. AND MRS. DUDDLEY, MR. DUDDLEY WAS BEST MAN AT THE CARTWRIGHT'S WEDDING TWENTY FIVE YEARS AGO, HE WAS MASTER OF CEREMONIES AT THEIR SILVER ANNIVERSARY THE CARTWRIGHT'S WERE MET AT THE DOOR BY THEIR DAUGHTER'S HOSTESS AND HOST

IN THE TRUE HAWAIIAN TRADITION WITH GREETINGS OF "ALOHA" LEIS PLACED AROUND THEIR NECKS.

THEY WERE THEN DRAPED IN GRASS SKIRTS, AND FLOWERS PLACED IN THEIR HAIR, HANDCUFFED TO ONE ANOTHER AND LED OFF TO MEET A CHORUS OF "ALOHAS" BEST WISHES FROM THEIR MANY FRIENDS ALL IN THE COLORFUL DRESS OF THE ISLAND.

A GAY TIME WAS HAD DANCING TO HAWAIIAN AND OLD TIME MUSIC, GAMES AND MUCH REMISING; AT MIDNIGHT A DELIGHTFUL LUNCH WAS SERVED.

Before leaving Dawn and Casey were presented with a palm tree, its branches and base were covered with centennial silver dollars. In case that should not grow they were given a genuine Hawaiian air plant, brought back from the Pacific Coast by Mr. & Mrs. Grover. By the time the party had ended it was twenty-five after three the next morning. When the Cartwright's had finally arrived home that morning, they were one very tired bunch. In the morning Blossom finally had gotten her horse from the riding academy, Casey bought a Blue Roan mare, standing fourteen hands high, the reason they had named the horse Blue Goose, Blossom was to find out later.

Well! you couldn't have seen a happier little girl than Blossom that morning, of course it had to rain when they were picking out just the right horse, Blossom had gotten all wet sitting on her horse, she had caught a cold, but she didn't care, she had finally gotten her horse.

The very next day the William's arrived at the Cartwright's around eleven PM. The following day when Sheila was offered a ride on the horse, she had to use a wooden carpenter's horse that you use to cut wood on, in order for her to step into the stirrups of the saddle on old Blue Goose. Was! that ever funny to watch a grown-up trying to get into the saddle that way. Sheila would have one person holding onto the reins and the other helping her to climb up into the saddle from the wooden horse. Every time Sheila tried to get into the saddle the old crafty horse would move just enough to one side, so she would loose her footing and fall between the wooden horse and old Blue Goose. That day everyone had a ride on the horse, the next day everyone went out to see the university sights from little mountain, except Cynthia. After seeing the university sights they all went out for dinner at the A & W restaurant.

The old Goose sure made the barn a helter skelter mess that evening. "Do you know Blossom and her dad were the only ones that would clean out that barn from one end to the other? Since the horse was bought, Blossom didn't really mind though, she knew the barn cleaning was going to be mostly her responsibility now, as well as her horse Blue Goose; to be scrubbed down all the time, the saddle and bridle well soaped down with saddle soap in order for it not to crack in the winter, it wasn't ordinary soap, you see it was a type of grease called saddle soap. While Blossom was still cleaning the barn her girl friend phoned again, that was a Monday afternoon, the next day she called Blossom, was on Thursday, Halloween night.

Willette went out dressed up as a hobo, Cynthia and Blossom stayed home with their parents giving out goodies, sometimes Casey would ask them to sing a song before handing the children any goodies.

They had been playing whist, a card game, when the first trick or theater came around. Blossom was getting good at whist by then; sometimes Casey would play for nickels or dimes with the family. After that she couldn't remember too much what all happened in her life until November in 1968, which was a Tuesday the thirteenth, Blossom recalls that day, because the Stewarts took her shopping at the new shopping mall. It was the first opening day of the shopping mall, after they spent all their money shopping, they came home, it was in the late afternoon, Dawn had dinner waiting on the table for all the guests, then Blossom did up the dishes, and watched some TV with her dad until 9:30, 10 o'clock that evening, the show was called "Route "66", it use to be her favorite program On November the nineteenth was a blank to Blossom, but on the twentieth she said, that she could remember that day real well, because Mrs. Stewart was over again helping Dawn wall papered her bedroom wall at the head of the twin beds, facing the west, the wall paper was a stripped olive green and lighter green. Blossom had been baking a chocolate cake while they were up stairs wall papering. Later she made a batch of chocolate half ways and a bunch of maple walnut bars, which she gave to Mrs. Stewart, a container full to take home to her family, I guess you could say my mother taught me to be generous as well as how to bake

In the next few days there was a lot of hustling around, Dolly phoned Blossom again to ask if she would like to go on a blind date with a fellow named Ruben. Blossom asked her dad if it was all right, she always asked one of her parents on any special occasion like that first, it was only proper in those days and showed respect to your parents. Only to Blossom's surprise, this time Casey said No, he wanted to be able to meet this Ruben fellow before she was aloud to go out with him. Casey then suggested phoning Dolly back and asking her to bring Ruben and her boy friend over to the house; they could take turns riding Old Blue Goose. In that way he could meet the young lad without him feeling like he was on display, dad could be pretty cagey some times.

Monday, Dawn went shopping again and bought Blossom a pair of fluffy pink bedroom slippers, While Blossom was out looking for a job again, she had walked about a mile or two in town looking for a job; and filling out application all day, she was really tired when her mom came home from shopping with her new slippers.

Blossom didn't have any luck with getting a secretary job in those days. It seemed that with her petit-mal no one but no one wanted to take a chance on hiring her. The following evening being Wednesday, Blossom went to night school again, doing her commercial art, Casey had driven her that evening, since Dawn and Mrs. Stewart had quit their typing course, that was held on the same evening at the same school, Cynthia was also taking a course then, she was taking a computer course that she did really well in, this was also held at the same school. Blossom made a Tokyo poster in class that evening. She had a lot of nice comments on her work from her classmates.

Saturday came around and it rained again, then the barn flooded and it rained some more, just like cats and dogs. Dolly phoned; when she was in the middle of cleaning the barn, she asked Blossom to go roller skating with Ruben and the rest of the bunch. She had just too much work and not enough play, so after she had finished her chores, she had her shower and went roller skating, enjoyed ever minute of it, when Blossom made up her mind there wasn't much you could do to change it. The very next day was something of a mystery to Blossom, since she had no record of what went on in those days, but on December the 2nd she did go Christmas shopping and bought Cynthia a beautiful black diamond necklace as a Christmas gift. With what Blossom earned in the strawberry field it wasn't a real diamond but it looked real enough. Then Mr. Stewart came over and helped Casey finish the basement on the new home. Monday December fifth, Blossom learned that a female fox was called a VIXON". Dawn's Birthday was the next day, Blossom had a special song dedicated to her mother on the radio for around one o'clock that afternoon, it was dedicated at that particular time of the day, because she knew Dawn would be home listening to that same radio station. The song was called "DON'T KNOW WHY I PUT UP WITH YOU", Dawn really liked that one, it was a funny song, Blossom thought it related to the way her mother felt about her.

The next days were spent getting ready for Christmas with all the trimmings that was a big time around our family. Being Thursday Dawn had decided to wash and set her short auburn hair; while Blossom was busy wrapping gifts, and helping her dad get the Christmas cards ready to be mailed, every year Casey would sit down at the old round oak dinning room table and pick out just the right Christmas card for each person on his list, then Dolly phoned Blossom again so they spent a short time getting all the latest gossip from each other, Dolly was Blossom's beast friend from school.

The following Saturday evening Clayton, one of Blossom's boy friends took her to the community hall for their annual Christmas dance. They arrived back home around 12 midnight after having such a terrific time, Dawn and Casey were still waiting up for her.

Sunday there was two sets of company invited for dinner at the Cartwright's home, they had quite a house full that evening around their old fashioned large oak dinning room table. Blossom hadn't been feeling too well that morning either, she was having quite a number of seizures again, she figured that could have been because of the late night she had the night before. Monday Clayton phoned up and wanted to take her out again that night, but Blossom knew that her parents wouldn't allow her to go out on a week night, when she had school the next day, only week ends. So Clayton promised that he would phone her back the following week end, Clayton kept his promise and phoned her back, then he arrived on her door step around eight-thirty all ready to take Blossom out again, Clayton was dressed real sharp in a dark suit and tie and long sleeve white shirt. They went out to a drive-in movie theatre near by. That evening with Clayton, Blossom had enjoyed herself so much that she had invited him back to the new years eve party her parents were putting on in their large finished rec-room down stairs, they had just finished about two months prior to the party, putting on the finishing touches. Blossom also had asked Dolly and her friend, Dolly is Clayton's sister the youngest of the sisters, but they had made other plans for New Years Eve. Clayton had been phoning Blossom quite a lot those days, He phoned her again that day, by the time they had said their good bye's he had surprised Blossom by calling her his "SWEET" Well! it was such a shock to her; it turned her head in many whirling directions. You see no one, but no one had ever called her his sweet before. Blossom had been getting lots of Christmas cards in the mail through the Christmas holidays. Being Christmas morning the family was still in their night wear except Casey, Casey was always dressed first thing in the morning, and it was usually just the women in the family that weren't dressed Christmas morning.

When Clayton arrived at the front door with a lovely wrapped gift of dusting powder and perfume for Blossom she was still in her house coat. After the session of opening presents, and! I do mean session, because it usually took anywhere from one to three hours with Casey playing Santa Clause, for everyone to open their presents, some of the presents were made by Dawn usually a dress or blouse for the girls. The tree was always a very bushy six foot tree that stood in a large picture window in the front living room.

The day after boxing day, Clayton and Blossom went out to another movie, this time they saw Gamet, after the movie he took her to a quaint little restaurant in the valley; where they had coffee and a hot dog, Blossom usually had pop or tea as she didn't like the taste of coffee, sometimes she would have white milk. That evening Clayton he kissed Blossom, the very first time, after dropping her off at the front door, then leaving for his home. He was very much a gentleman.

Blossom; while she was asleep in her double bed she had dreamt about Clayton and her very first kiss with him. The following Wednesday all the Cartwright's went visiting their Uncle Dudley, except Blossom, she stayed home grooming her horse which she loved more than air its self. Blossom had a great love for animals; she said they don't hurt your feelings like people do.

Sheila phoned long distance that evening while Blossom was still home alone. To let them know they would be arriving in by CP AIR on the following Friday the Thirteenth at one-fifteen in the afternoon, could someone please come to pick them up at the airport? Then Clayton phoned again to say that he would be coming to the New Years Eve party after all. That New Years Eve party was sure a lot of fun for everyone, said Blossom, as she leaned back in her rocking chair to rock a little more. It had ended around two thirty-three in the morning, drinking and dancing and having a good old fashioned time. Blossom had to watch that she didn't have too much liquor or her seizures would start up all over again, sometimes worse than the time before. Dawn didn't like her to drink at all, but Casey would give Blossom some once in awhile. At the party Clayton and Blossom had to dance against three other couples on the floor in a contest, each with a balloon between their foreheads without dropping the balloon in order to win one of the nicely wrapped gifts that Dawn had for them. The object to the game was to see who could dance the longest with a balloon between their foreheads; before they dropped the balloon on the floor. At the end of the dance the balloon that was between Clayton and Blossom's foreheads ended up balancing between their nose and their frames of their glasses. Clayton and Blossom won the game and the prizes it was some perfumed soap for Blossom and a deck of playing cards for Clayton, Dawn was hoping that her friends would have won. As Blossom was telling the story she got a little teary eyed when she came to the part about her mother, Blossom had always felt left out when it came to her sisters and her mother, it was ok on a one to one bases, but when they all got together she always felt that they didn't want her around.

After the dance was all finished, Dawn was quite up set with Blossom, since she had refused to loose the contest just so Dawn's friends would win. Blossom could be quite stubborn when she wanted to be, especially when she thought people were being unfair to her or her friends, Blossom's feelings were quite easily hurt, but she usually kept them hidden so no one would see her cry, many a times she said she would lie awake in her bed a night crying silently, because she had felt unwanted by her family. That year was quite a good year for Blossom and in the next few months to come was to be even better.

Chapter Seven

Blossom's Engagement

In the days to come, Blossom seizures were slowly slowing down. She was now off any medication that she might have been on in the past. On Monday Blossom was invited out to Isabel's home with Randal, there was Bois and Alfred who were all ready there, Bois being a bit of a bully picked a fight with Alfred, who was a very shy person. By the time that Blossom had arrived, Alfred had ended up with a bloody nose, the blood was just pouring out all over his favorite dress shirt and face. Alfred had been trying to hold the blood back with the palm of his hands so his hands were also covered in blood. That's when one of the other's took him to the hospital for stitches. Clayton felt sorry for Blossom; since she was suppose to be Alfred's date, He decided to ask Blossom out to a movie since his brother Alfred couldn't. It would help her to forget about the terrible fight she had just witnessed.

After the movie Clayton took Blossom out to a Chinese restaurant for a delicious dinner and then home. By then Blossom had found herself a job working in a green house, the pay wasn't much but it was a job, "thought Blossom". Being this a Friday, Blossom received her pay cheque, every Friday was pay day then on every Friday after work she would put so much in the bank and so much of her pay cheque towards the china dinner set, and piece by piece Blossom finally got the complete set of eight. Clayton phoned her again the following day and they talked that afternoon for some time. Blossom would take the down stairs phone in the hallway the cord was long enough she could take it into the bathroom and lock the door for privacy. Clayton phoned to see if she would like to go with him the following weekend for a drive up the mountain. Blossom looked forward for the opportunity to be able to go out again with Clayton in the mountains. That same afternoon Lynn, one of Blossom's kind hearted girl friends from grade school, a couple of years back, Lynn came down to tell Blossom that she had heard through the grape vine Clayton's younger brother wanted to take Blossom out one night, but he was too shy to ask her for a date. Blossom wasn't busy that day so Lynn and she went down town shopping. Blossom had bought the longest pair of white gloves she had ever seen. She was getting kind of worried since she hadn't seen or heard from Clayton all week. Isabelle still had Blossom's record player and records that she had borrowed awhile back, Blossom thought for a minute and decided that she would use that as a good reason to visit Isabelle's brother Clayton. They lived on a dairy farm a few miles away. You see she wanted to see for herself if Clayton had found a new girl friend. Clayton was calling Blossom at least once a day and then all of a sudden he stopped calling. By the time she arrived over there Blossom was still trying to find away to ask Clayton why he hadn't phoned her or at least come over for awhile, but she didn't want to seem too pushy. Blossom then listened to Isabelle for awhile about her brother and then decided to try and get Clayton's attention. The following Saturday Blossom took the old horse went out for a very long ride as she often did, they would stop in at a small town corner grocery store and cafeteria combination, this store was located on the corner by the elementary school yard, there she would tether up old Blue Goose while purchasing a single apple for her horse as a treat.

    Before they went back home Blossom would feed the apple to the old Blue Goose, it was sort of a reward for being a good horse on the long ride.

    As Blossom was about to mount her horse she had met a handsome young man which she had gone to school with him; in junior high school a couple of years before. Only Blossom at the time didn't remember him being at the same school as she, you see he wasn't in the same class, he was in a higher grade.

    Blossom thought, "He was kind of rugged looking in the face, he hadn't shaved for a couple of days, "This young man was wearing his motorcycle black leather jacket that was only half zipped up. As Blossom looked him up and down describing every little feature in her mind and remember it, she heard him say something, which was being directed in her direction, not knowing quite what he had said, she just said Hello. That young rugged attractive man had thought Blossom had being speaking to him. Not realizing she was only answering him back, he didn't want to be rude, so he came over and introduced himself as Wesley. Wesley and Blossom got to talking and in that conversation she had discovered a lot about him, like for one thing, "he hadn't been talking to her just then," he had been calling out to his father who had just drove by in the old Model A with a crank on the front, that was incase it didn't want to start you would have to get out of the car and crank it until the car would start again, In time Blossom was to find this out. As they were talking Blossom could feel him giving her the once over from the tip of her black cowboy boots that were almost worn out, to the top of her fair colored hair full of curlers.

Blossom's figure wasn't too bad back then; she could still fit into a two piece swim suit, as he was looking her up and down, she felt sorry for Wesley he had missed his ride home, but she knew that the old horse wouldn't double, so she couldn't offer him a ride home on her horse, with out thinking she just blurted it out and asked him if he would like to try riding the old horse around the block by himself Well! That was a funny sight to see. Wesley no sooner had gotten his foot in the stirrup, when the old horse just took off like a bolt of lightening.

It was such a funny sight; Blossom just couldn't help but laugh out loud, only after he was out of hearing range. When Wesley came back from his ride, he asked Blossom if she would like to go out with him, if he could get his father's car for the evening. Thinking that was a strange way to ask for a date with a girl he had just met, but thinking that he would be kind of nice to go out with, Blossom decided to play it cool by saying, "she would have to first ask her parents permission, that not really being a lie she had taken Isabelle's advice.

Blossom had now started to play hard to get, you see she didn't want Wesley to think that she was ready to jump into any man's lap, which was true Blossom wouldn't do that anyway. In the next few seconds Blossom found herself giving him her phone number to be sure that he would phone her back; when and if he could get his father's car for the evening. Wesley promised to phone Blossom, but she figured that she really wouldn't hear from him again. After Blossom had arrived home late that afternoon, she didn't bother to mention about the young man she had just met, unless Wesley really did phone her back. Blossom had just finished taking her curlers out of her long ash blonde hair, when a storm started to brew up and the old horse was starting to act up in the pasture, you can always tell when there's a storm on it's way, when the animals start acting up.

She had to run outside right away to bring her horse, the sheep and the dogs in the barn. All Blossom did was just take the last curler out of her hair, it still wasn't combed out properly. Blossom had to try and catch that old Blue Goose before her horse tried to knock anymore fences down. Her horse wasn't an easy horse to catch and she was having a hard time of it. Casey saw from the kitchen window the hard time Blossom was having and came out to give her a hand. Once they both finally caught that crafty old horse, Blossom curried and rubbed down Blue Goose real well, "it felt real good from the long hard ride that afternoon, "she thought that must be what her horse was thinking.

See if you don't rub a horse down real good after a hard ride, the horse could easily become sick, but Blossom knew enough not to give Blue Goose water (ice water) until old Blue had stopped sweating.

About one or two hours after she was all finished, Blossom ran back into the house before the rains started to come.

After having a refreshing shower and something to eat for dinner, then helping to clear the dinner dishes away real fast as though something was going on that evening, but Blossom still hadn't told her parents she was expecting a phone call from a young man, when they asked she just told them she didn't like to see a messy kitchen, which was true enough. It wasn't long after Blossom had sat down and started to knit, when she had forgotten something up stairs in the bedroom, just as she reached the top of the stair case on her way back down, the phone rang, being Cynthia walking by the phone at that moment, she answered it. It was Wesley just like he had promised her, "Hello, "says Cynthia, in her deep very sexy voice. "Can I speak to Mary says Wesley". "Mary" Cynthia say's," there's no Mary living here." "You must have the wrong number." Wesley came back quickly saying, "are you sure there is no Mary living there?" Yes said Cynthia, "what number are you calling?" The number was correct. Well! Wesley thought for a minute and then said. "Let me speak to the girl who just rode in on the old Goose," Laughed Cynthia as she said Oh! You mean Blossom," that's it Wesley answered in a relieved voice. "Wesley could remember the horses name but not Blossom's. At that moment she called up to Blossom who was still at the top of the stairs just outside her parent's bedroom door. Blossom took the call in her parent's bedroom. After Cynthia had hung up the phone down stairs, she had only then started to talk to Wesley. Blossom was shocked to hear it was really him after all. That's when she finally asked her parents for the first time that evening if she could go out with Wesley, for the evening. At first while they were all sitting in the living room by the bay window just relaxing and talking over the events of the day. Casey and Dawn were reluctant to let Blossom go out again, since she was out late the night before. Blossom still hadn't gotten over her petit-mal; she needed a lot more sleep than most teenagers.

Casey had thought, "he should of met this young man first, but Cynthia saved the evening for Blossom, by speaking up and saying that she knew Wesley from high school and he is a real nice guy.

Wesley picked Blossom up around eight o'clock on the dot that evening, asked her what drive-in movie she would like to see, Wesley gave Blossom two choices, she had seen them both before, So Wesley picked the drive-in movie they would see, only at that time he didn't know that Blossom had all ready seen them both before.

In order not to hurt Wesley's feelings Blossom just kept quiet about seeing the movie with her date the night before. After they had been at the drive-in for a short time, Wesley reached over to Blossom and gave her a kiss, at first he just bent his head half way over as to kiss her and then he stopped dead in his tracks. Blossom was wondering by now why he had stopped dead in his tracks, she thought maybe she had bad breath or something, then he came closer and when their two lips finally did meet it was just like the fourth of July. Boy! Their chemicals were sure just right at that moment in time, Blossom finally found out what her mother had been telling her all those years that you will know when you meet Mr. Right.

That first kiss set rockets off for both Wesley and Blossom, you don't really know what it is like until it has happened to you, then you know no matter what ever else happens to you he/she is still the one that the good Lord had sent down from Heaven to you until death do you part. Blossom believed then and still does believe that was the way God was telling her that Wesley was her Mr. Right.

After the first kiss, it started to rain and rain in buckets full, Wesley made a mad dash to the concessionary stand to purchase one of the cardboard rain visors, in which in those days you could purchase them for fifty cents for the car. "You never had seen anyone run so fast as Wesley did that evening." When he came back with the rain visors about five minutes later he had a grin from ear to ear. They sat close together all evening watching the movie, but not before Wesley tried to make out with Blossom in the front seat of his daddy's model "A" car. She soon showed him that she was not that sort of a girl and he had respected her for it every since. On the way back home they stopped in at the drive-in restaurant and ordered two large glasses of milk, Blossom had fallen asleep on Wesley's shoulder by then, so the girl hop only tapped on the car window to take their order. By the time the order arrived Wesley had very gently woken Blossom up. When it was time to leave Wesley drove over to the restaurant door where the girl hop would come out to pick up the empty trays, he wanted to save her a few steps, but when he drove over there, one large glass had dropped and broke, glass all over their parking lot, you see his window wouldn't stay up all the time, and with the weight of the tray resting on it; made the window come down.

On the way back to Blossom's home that evening Wesley wanted to see what kind of a girl she really was like; that he had fallen in love with. Wesley pulled into Blossom's long driveway and came to a stop in front of the Cartwright's carport, there he came on pretty strong with a pass after he kissed her one more time on her delicious strawberry lips. As Wesley was kissing Blossom for the third time, Dawn turned on the front spot light, it shown right into the front seat that meant time was up and come inside now. He soon found out that Blossom was a decent young lady, not a nice girl, in those days a nice girl was one who goes to bed and then goes home, at least that was what the boys would call a girl like that. By the time that Wesley had walked Blossom to her front door, he had all ready proposed to her. It came as a real surprise to Blossom for Wesley to purpose marriage to her on their very first date together. Blossom just decided to tell him politely, but tactfully that she wasn't about to jump into a relationship on her very first date with him or any other man. When Wesley suggested that they could get better acquainted first, she bluntly told him, "Wesley your off your rocker," In that note Wesley decided to see what would happen if he carried that particular conversation further with her, he had hinted that they should go some place and have sex, as if Blossom would get right down to the nitty gritty right then and there. "NOT!" On that remark Blossom just slipped quietly into the house and Wesley had to go home. In the days to come Blossom was starting to fall in love with Wesley and Wesley had all ready fallen for Blossom quite hard in fact. She had all ready told Cynthia that evening about the proposal of marriage he gave her.

The very first thing Cynthia said, "Your not going to marry him, are you? Blossom didn't know at the time. After about the first couple of dates with Wesley, Blossom had told him about her petit-mal and the seizures that she gets, he was so very understanding with Blossom when ever she had one of her seizures, in fact sometimes he would get very worried if they lasted longer than usual. Then one evening Blossom had a fight with Casey; and Cynthia, it was more like just being fed up with everything she just walked out. Blossom had enough blames when it wasn't always her fault. She walked right out the front door, about eight O'clock that evening. Blossom walked and walked hoping to cool down, then decided to see Wesley at his place of employment, she knew where he worked, it was a cabinet shop, but not exactly how to get there, it was pitch dark out by then, Blossom was a little afraid to be walking in the dark by herself, the streets weren't lit up too well, not like now a days. He worked about ten miles from where she lived, so brave Blossom was only wearing a thin jacket to keep warm and walking towards the direction of Wesley's work. In her walk she had passed a police car parked on the side of the road facing the opposite direction in which she had been walking. There were two male officers sitting in the front seat, it looked as though they were writing something down. Blossom wasn't even three car lengths from the police car, when she stopped in her tracks, she had just spotted Wesley's car going home, he drove right pass her not even seeing Blossom on the side of the road.

By that time Dawn and Casey were all ready looking for her. They had phoned their friends close by to see if she had gone down there first, but there was no Blossom. Blossom decided to turn around after thinking the situation over first very carefully and headed back home to be where she knew there was security and love.

As Wesley was all ready home anyway, thought Blossom, there was no use for her to keep walking, it was useless to walk in the dark and pretty soon it was going to get colder. Besides she had a job to go to tomorrow; in the mean time Blossom didn't know that the police officers were keeping a close watch on her, when she turned around to go home, they drove over in their black and white police car to where she stood confused, the officers started to question Blossom, the first officer asked her name and address and where she was going so late at night. She gave her name and address to the officers and told them she usually goes out for long walks in the evening by herself. When Blossom had gotten almost home, Casey and Dawn pulled up from behind her and told her to get into the car; they had been out looking for Blossom for some time then. Dawn had been worried about Blossom and her seizures, Blossom wouldn't get into the car then, she was still quite upset with them, then Dawn said the same thing in a nicer tone of voice, but Blossom still refused to go into that car, so Casey just drove back home without her. He still was quite upset with Blossom and Blossom was still upset with him and Cynthia.

Blossom walked a little further, then Wesley came up from the back with his old beat up red and white Chevy car, he had bought a year before. Wesley was quite worried then explained to her, that he had gone straight over to see her after work; before changing out of his grubby work clothes, when he had heard that Blossom was missing. Wesley started looking for her. He looked in every bar and hotel in town and to any other place that he could think of that Blossom might have gone to.

By the time Wesley finally finished telling her how worried he was, Blossom was in the front seat feeling very safe. Wesley wanted Blossom to go home and make up with her parents, but she refused and with that he took her for a bit of a drive until she had calmed down enough to go back home, Blossom thought her parents would still be waiting up for her, but they had gone to bed and were fast asleep.

Blossom felt kind of stupid now from the whole episode and didn't want to face her parents that evening, she knew in the morning she was going to have to face them and that would be soon enough. Wesley told Blossom that the next time she wanted to run away from home, she should go over to his place and wait for him there, he still lived at home with his family too, but Blossom never did try to run away from home again.

Blossom was nineteen at the time an average looking girl. The very next weekend Wesley came over and took Blossom out for a nice drive in the country, that was the drive Blossom loved the most, alone with Wesley in the calm of the country-side. They both loved the drive in the country, especially in the fall months when the leaves were just turning different colors. Different times when Blossom would do something that she knew would make Wesley mad, he would try and keep calm, but she would do it anyway, just in order to get a little affection in her life, her life was pretty lonely until Wesley came along. Oh! Sure she had boy friends, but they usually only wanted one thing.

The first time Wesley ever laid eyes on Blossom; he wanted to take her out then, that was when Blossom was in her strawberry stained white blouse, shorts and running shoes with curlers in her blonde hair, delivering baskets of strawberries to one of her mother's elderly customers at their home. Wesley had been raking the hay out in the back field, to him Blossom looked quite cute in her strawberry stained outfit. As Wesley remembers that very first time, it was a year before he had actually met Blossom on her horse. Wesley was still very patient with Blossom even though he was having a hard time holding back that evening, but Blossom had other ideas, she was determined to be married a virgin. When the time came for Wesley to make his move, Blossom took out her hair pin shaped like a sword, glittering of rhinestones placed on a sliver like substance, in the moon light. Blossom then started to poke Wesley's arm. Really she had no intentions of hurting him, but she had thought that if she could scare him a little bit, it just might cool him down awhile, it worked! Wesley was very upset with her as he caught her hand in time, and darn near broke her right arm. After that Blossom got out of the car and started down the back alley towards the entrance. You see Dawn and Casey never had too much time to spend on Blossom with the other three girls to look after, and there were certain things Blossom couldn't do, because of her petit-mal. Dawn was in a constant worry about if Blossom should not do this or that, and now there was their grandchildren to consider too, they needed to spend time with them. One time Blossom went with Wesley out to a late movie on a Friday evening after work, it was a near by drive-in; then at the end of the movie Wesley asked Blossom if she would like to go for a drive in the country. Blossom loved to go for a drive in the country and was very pleased for the opportunity, only he took her to lover's lane instead, about three miles from the drive-in. There were only a few homes on that alleyway; it was where all the lovers parked after midnight, so they named it lover's lane. That particular evening the moon was at its fullest shinning down on Blossom's radiant face and golden hair. Wesley had just stopped the car and couldn't hold back any longer, he had been waiting to make love to Blossom for over a year now, she would always manage to stop him. You see she wanted to save herself for their wedding night. Blossom didn't want to and had a fight with Wesley, by then she had been crying for so long, that a elderly gentleman came running out from inside his home to see if he could help this girl in any way. He had thought that Blossom was in some kind of trouble out there, like maybe this fellow was trying to rape her or worse, he had really come down on Wesley, by then Blossom was feeling so ashamed of herself making such a fuss that the elderly kind gentleman had to come running out in his slippers to rescue her from Wesley, then giving Wesley a good balling out. He almost called the police on him, but that didn't stop Blossom from testing Wesley's love for her, you see Blossom never had a secure feeling outside her parent's home.

    Finally Wesley calmed Blossom down enough to get her back into the car and then apologized, but Blossom was only in long enough to reach the entrance, when all of a sudden she tried to jump out of the car, while the car was still in slow motion, ready to stop at a T intersection. Blossom didn't really want to jump, but she wanted to see if Wesley would try and pull her back in the car, which of course he did. Blossom only knew one way to get attention and that was the wrong way. Poor Wesley he loved Blossom so much, yet he just didn't know how to tell her that he didn't know how to deal with her in those depressed moods. Then there was the time when she was at her old tricks again, Blossom would say," this time she pretended to faint in Wesley's arms." She really ever fainted, but there was one time Blossom remembered when she really did faint, it was the time she had such a bad ear infection, the whole family was up at their uncle cottage on the lake, but that was another story, Getting back to the time she pretended to faint in Wesley's arms, they were in the front seat of his old Chevy, it was parked on the gravel road outside of his parents home, a isolated gravel road. Blossom held her breath; you see she knew that Wesley would think she had stopped breathing, that maybe she would have frightened him enough to give him the message that she was trying so hard to tell him all this time. She didn't like anything around her neck, especially anyone's hands. Blossom felt sorry for Wesley after he had tried to give her mouth to mouth resuscitation, but that was the only way Blossom knew to get the message across to him from ever doing it again.

Wesley was very shocked that Blossom had stopped breathing, at least he had thought at the time she did, Wesley figured the one he loved so very much had just died in his arms, He gave Blossom mouth to mouth resuscitation until she couldn't hold her breath any longer.

Blossom can still remember what she had been thinking, "How am going to get myself out of this mess now, "I got myself into this, without Wesley thinking that I was just playing a game on him." You see if Wesley knew that Blossom was just playing one of her tricks again, he would have been madder than a wet hen in heat. After what seemed an awful long time to Wesley, trying to bring Blossom back to life, Blossom decided to come out of it gradually.

The look! on Wesley's face was priceless, he had the look of a man who just brought his loved one back to life, that was a look that no one could explain That scare smartened Wesley up; he never put his hands around her neck again, since anything around Blossom's neck has made her feel like she can't breath, ever since the time Sheila had tried to choke her years ago.

Casey and Dawn were out for their Sunday drive looking at houses, they liked to do that, Cynthia was sitting next to Blossom in the den down stairs, when Sheila started to choke Blossom by putting her hands around Blossom's throat and shaking her, Cynthia didn't even try to stop Sheila from choking Blossom, and she was sitting right beside Blossom on the couch. It was Willette who finally came down stairs and seen what was happening then stopped Sheila, Cynthia tried to stop Willette from stopping her then, and that was why Blossom didn't like anything around her neck.

Back to Wesley, after that session he took Blossom in his arms ever so gently and kissed her and apologized over and over again to her, then kissed her on the peak of her shinny little nose once again.

In the next summer to come Wesley got to meet the rest of Blossom's family, the first one he met was her older sister Sheila and her husband Grant with their two children Sheldon the eldest and Betty the baby.

Almost ever other night Wesley would come over and play with Sheldon and Betty, who were five and three at the time. Wesley loved little children very much, he had taken a liking to the children, Betty and Sheldon both took a great liking to him too. One evening after work Wesley picked Blossom up from the green house where she was working for the past three years, like he had done many times before, only this time he had also picked up a hitch-hiker, in fact Wesley gave him the car keys to drive while he sat in the middle of the front seat, Blossom on the other side of him. Wesley had hit a pot hole on his way back from work, he had a couple of co-workers in the car with him, the car went out of control and they almost got into an accident, this shook Wesley up so much he didn't want to drive. So when they picked up Blossom the hitch-hiker was driving his car. Blossom hadn't had her drivers license as of yet. She was sitting next to Wesley; was thinking about their very first date, when Wesley asked her to marry him and she had told him he was off his rocker. She had just heard a few days earlier from one of her girl friends that Wesley had also asked the same question to one of the other girls a year before he had met Blossom, there was one way for Blossom to figure out if he really meant what he had said on their very first date. Blossom had asked Wesley to repeat what he had asked her that evening they went out together, right then in the car with the hitch-hiker as a witness. She didn't give him any hints about what she was talking about, because if he really meant it, that he wanted to marry her, then she figured that Wesley would have remembered what he had asked her then. When Wesley repeated the proposal, Blossom surprised him by saying yes. They didn't tell her parents right away as Blossom wanted to surprise them when she received her engagement ring. Which to come in a couple of months down the line; when Wesley could afford it. This was March and by September the month of Blossom's birthday, Wesley had bought the engagement ring after searching with Blossom for along time and not coming up with the right one, they were either too big or too expensive, she didn't want Wesley to spend a lot of money on her ring.

Wesley picked out a tiny ring, white gold with a gold band and three tiny diamonds mounted so dainty in a pyramid style. They courted for two years which seemed very long to Blossom, before they had gotten married, a lot had happened back then, in those two years.

The day Wesley placed the engagement ring on Blossom's third finger of her left hand; she was fast asleep on the hide-a-bed in the den on the main floor of the Cartwright's new home. After that Blossom use to use soap and water to get the tiny ring off before going to work in the morning to the green house, until one day Wesley took the ring back to the jewelry store to be enlarged.

Two very long years of being courted in the most promising way, Wesley picked Blossom up every evening from work after he finished his construction work across town, then he would either take her out to dinner after they both had a chance to clean up, or they would have dinner at his parent's home. Most of the time Wesley was invited over to the Cartwright's for dinner.

On one occasion Wesley had picked Blossom up from work and then at six-thirty they went out to visit his younger brother Rob and his wife Laura, Laura's nick name was Blossom, since when they found out that Blossom's birth name was Blossom, Laura went back to being called Laura again. Rob and Laura had a son called Jason about a month old. Blossom and Wesley would stay a short time visiting, then the following day Wesley would pick up Blossom and they would go shopping. He'd take Blossom out to jewelry shops and women's wear shops to see what he could buy for her, but she always thought that they were too expensive and said so. On Sunday the two of them would go to church at the church in the valley, after church services Blossom and Wesley would always go for a long drive in the country while the sun was still shinning.

Sometimes they came back to the Cartwright's home after church, have lunch ready for the entire family to sit around the large oak dinning room table. On those occasions the family would play card games, Wesley loved to play card games with her parents.

Occasionally Wesley would pick Blossom up after work, they would go out to an evening movie, and usually it was a Friday evening when they didn't have to go to work the next morning. Being a Friday Wesley picked Blossom up and as usual they went to a drive-in-movie, they would cuddle while watching the movie. Then by two a.m. he always had Blossom home in time for her curfew set by her parents. Saturday the two of them packed a picnic lunch and picked up some friend's then headed off to the hot springs. Well! It started to rain and I mean rain in buckets full. By then the couple in the back had wished they had never came and asked Wesley to drive them back home, He turned the car around and dropped them off each at their own homes, then Wesley and Blossom went out to the country for another drive, never got home until late that evening.

Sometimes they would take little Betty and Sheldon with them in the country. One day Wesley was on his way out the kitchen door from the Cartwright's home when Betty out of the blue asked her mom in a quiet voice if that man was going to stay for dinner too. It was beginning to be a habit with Blossom asking Wesley over for dinner, He finally decided that it was time he had dinner at his own home for a change and not to over stay his welcome at the Cartwright's home. Betty thought he had lived there too. Oh! How I remember Betty she was such a wonderful child, so full of life.

When the summer came around that year Betty and Sheldon would be playing in the unfenced back yard near the finished fish pond, At the Cartwright's home while the rest of the family and sometimes Wesley would help out with picking those strawberries to get them ready for market After all the berries were picked for the day, Dawn would treat the family out for a milk shake from the Dairy Queen, it usually was chocolate mostly asked for. On one occasion the berries were all finished being picked and graded into baskets for the day, it was about one in the afternoon, since it was much too hot for any more strawberry picking that Saturday afternoon. Wesley took Blossom out to the country beach for a wonderful refreshing swim, "Did that water ever feel good and refreshing after a long morning in the hot sticky berry fields. The water was swishing up against their lily white bodies as Blossom was trying to teach Wesley how to swim. Blossom loved to go swimming there; it was so peaceful usually just the two of them, once in awhile you would see a sailing ship in the distance against the blue sky. Wesley had to lead the way before you could reach the beach; they were climbing up and down the winding rough trail in the bush that led down to the beach. That particular afternoon they were joking around after having a terrific time in the water, Wesley had carried Blossom over the rocks to where the trail exit started, when he fell with her at the base of the hill, Thank God they weren't hurt said Blossom, You see you had to cross the railway tracks before you got to the base of the trail, when they fell. Wesley found something shinny sticking partly out of the sandy soil, He dug it out of the sandy soil with his fingers and discovered it to be a women's ring. That ring had two rubies mounted one on either side of the culture pearl placed on a band of gold. Blossom and Wesley being very honest people had put an ad in the local paper the following day, but by the time the week was up for the ad no one had answered it. So Wesley took that little ring down to the jewelry store in town the next morning to have it enlarged to fit Blossom's finger, at the same time he had the ring analyzed, You know that ring was worth twenty-five dollars back then.

    Back then Sheila would have to fly Betty and Sheldon to the coast in order to be able to take Betty to the children's hospital, while Sheldon would stay with Grandma Cartwright. Since out on the Island where they lived there wasn't proper equipment for the tests that Betty needed to have done. Betty needed lots of tests done; on her little body. Sheila and Grant moved out to the Island about a year before when Grant was transferred from his job at the airlines on the coast. Sometimes Betty would be in the hospital for months at a time. While Betty was in the hospital for a period of a long time the rest of the family would be staying at the Cartwright's home where Dawn had a special room all fixed up with a crib and a bed for the three of them. You see Grant couldn't make it down to the coast with his family all the time. Grant would have to stay on the Island and work in order to pay for the hospital bills, they couldn't afford for him to take too much time off work, but they would phone once a week to each other and Sheila would let Grant know what kind of progress Betty was making.

    Little Betty had leukemia from a very early age of two; she was spending most of her life in and out of the children's hospital. She was a very beautiful little girl, the spitting image of her mother in the face. Her hair was long about to the middle of her back; usually put up in a pony tail fashion, it use to shine like star dust in the summer. Then came the day, the day everyone will remember, it was a very warm summer afternoon on a Tuesday. Blossom remembers the day well, she had been working that afternoon in the green house in the month of May, all the daffodils were out in bloom and the blue birds were all singing away in their summer songs, just like all the summers that are beautiful, like the ones you read in fairy tail story books Blossom was working in the green house building, amongst the carnations and the plants that were left over from Easter. It was at the furthest end of the green house, plants and flowers always lasted a couple of months after the day they were due. Blossom was getting them prepared for the local flower shop in town.

Around four-thirty, quitting time just like the other days, Wesley would pick her up on the roadside as it was too muddy to drive in. She would be waiting for him out on the road, just like many times before. Only that day he had a different look on his face, kind of like a far away look, and yet that didn't really explain the look either, it was hard to describe the look on Wesley's face that afternoon.

Blossom thought that maybe she just better keep quiet until he was ready to tell her what was bothering him, only he didn't say anything, it was a very quiet drive home. When she arrived home, Dawn told her that afternoon Betty had just passed away about one o'clock in the afternoon in the children's hospital bed.

Dawn had been looking after Sheldon while Sheila was visiting in the hospital with Betty that tragic afternoon. Just before Betty had passed away, she sat straight up in her hospital bed and looked to the right of her out the large picture window where the sun was shinning down on her golden hair, opened up her bright blue eyes and called for Sheldon, then she quietly passed away into Heaven.

Apparently when Betty had called out for Sheldon many miles away, Sheldon told Grandma that he heard Betty calling to him. Sheldon was only five at the time, so being so very young Grandma Cartwright didn't believe him. Sheldon and Betty were very close sister and brother growing up.

The funereal was held three days later in a little chapel on the hillside in the country where Betty was laid to rest beneath an evergreen tree that shaded her little grave in the cemetery.

Sheila and Grant never cried once the whole time the ceremony was going on, some of the people could say that it wasn't good for them to bottle it all up inside themselves, like they were doing. That afternoon the Cartwright's had their home open for relatives and friends to come and pay their respects to Sheila and Grant.

Dawn had asked Wesley to take Blossom out because she was afraid that Blossom might black out and say something wrong, little did they know that she was very upset too about the whole ordeal and wanted to give her condolences to Sheila and Grant too, but Dawn asked her stay away from Sheila and Grant who were in the kitchen with the doors shut trying to understand why Betty had to die so young.

In the next couple of days everything was almost back to normal in the Cartwright's home. Sheila and Grant took Sheldon and left for their home on the Island, only this time their hearts were empty loosing their only beloved daughter. Then came the day when Wesley let the cat out of the bag, it was about one year later, he had asked Blossom's father for her hand in marriage. Wesley just wanted Casey's permission for now, later when they could afford to get married they would. Wesley brought the engagement ring over to Blossom, it was the day before the Cartwright's had decided to go to the lake where their Uncle Jed owned a cabin.

The Cartwright's had just purchased a travel trailer; Wesley had driven Blossom up after picking up some medication for her ear infection. That evening the women all spent the night in the trailer while the men slept in the cabin, Blossom had the top bunk just above her parents bed, it was so hot up there she had a hard time sleeping, also she was taking ear drops and aspirin every half hour as the night proceeded on. Her ear infection was getting worse. Blossom didn't want to go up to the lake with the rest of her family, but Dawn told her earlier that they wouldn't go up there without her, she wanted to please them.

The next morning Blossom had gotten up to use the travel trailer's bathroom, she wasn't dressed yet, when Dawn stopped her and said, "I don't want you to use the bathroom here, Use the one inside the cabin," I want this one to keep clean, it has to be dumped later, "So first Blossom had to get all dressed up before going into the cabin of men. When she arrived at the front door just inside the kitchen she fainted right in front of the door and in front of the fridge which was next to the sink in which you had to bucket the water in. On the other side of the sink was the wood burning stove, black in color. It was hot enough to heat the whole cabin. As you walked into the dinning room area the living room was straight ahead.

To the left of the living room one single bedroom and just along aside the bedroom was the bathroom. There was a patio to the right of the living room with a large picture window over looking the lake. The walls were all unpainted just like the floors all wood. Blossom's Uncle Jed found her passed out on the floor.

Wesley ended up taking Blossom about three hours earlier home than the rest of the Cartwright family. As her ear was in more pain than before, but only not before her Uncle Jed had found Blossom lying on the kitchen floor, he had brought a glass of water over for her for when she awoke. Then he escorted her over to the couch on the other side of the living room. Blossom sat there half awake while she waited patiently to get into the bathroom.

On the following Thursday Wesley and Blossom went into town to shop, didn't get back home until ten in the evening. Then in the next evening Wesley took Blossom out to another out-door movie to see "Doctor Speaks Out," That show was all about having babies, it was all worth seeing again, said Blossom as she remembers back in her earlier years.

Saturday Blossom had a dentist appointment which Casey took her to. When they had gotten back Wesley was in the drive-way waiting to take her to the States with him. They spent the rest of the day in the States, and then came home all tired from shopping. When they arrived back home at the Cartwright's late that afternoon Grant's younger brother and his girl friend were waiting for them. Next day being a Sunday the four of them took off to the beach to get some swimming in before her friends had to go back to the valley. What! A lot of fun they all had that afternoon, remembers Blossom as she gets up from her rocking chair to make tea. The four of them had supper at the beach, they had roasted weenies and had potato salad and chips with canned pop, while sitting around a camp fire telling stories. Around eleven in the evening they all packed up to go back to the Cartwright's home all tired out. His girl friend slept with Blossom while Larry slept in the Cartwright's travel trailer out back.

One afternoon Wesley took Blossom fishing up at the fisherman cove about forty miles in the bush He loved to fish, but Blossom wasn't much of a fisherman, she tried very hard to enjoy herself for Wesley's sake. The sun was shinning quite warmly that afternoon down on her golden curls, but some how she couldn't get the hang of fishing. When they arrived home just after four in the afternoon with a arm full of trout, Wesley gave all of the fish to Dawn to cook up for supper, she asked him to stay for supper, but only after he cleaned the fish, she would say It was a lot of fun back in those days; everything was sunshine and roses to the ones that were in love for the very first time.

Chapter Eight

The Year She Concord the Invisible Foe

Blossom was now twenty-one years of age and finally grown out of her Petit-Mal, that was the happiest time in her life. She knew she was one of the lucky ones, because not everyone who has epilepsy gets to out grow it.

Ever since she could remember, her dream was to someday concord that epilepsy, that Invisible Foe as Blossom would call it, it was hanging over her head for seventeen long years and she was at last finally finished with it, every birthday and every prayer she ever had was to someday get rid of the epilepsy. Once when Blossom saw a falling star she wished upon it that someday her petit-mal would go away and never come back again.

Wesley had taken Blossom out to celebrate her victory in the evening, after the celebration he had taken her to his home. His parents were all ready gone out, so they had the whole house to themselves. He took her by the hand ever so gently Wesley took Blossom up to his sister's bedroom, it was larger than Wesley's and had a large double bed, her room was just across from Wesley's tiny bedroom. Wesley ever so gently laid Blossom in the middle of the down filled double bed, then made beautiful passionate love to the women he loved and had planned on marrying someday This was the very first time for Blossom, and the very first time in almost two years for the two of them together. Blossom finally had given herself to Wesley totally; this was the man she was going to marry.

It wasn't exactly what Blossom had thought the first time would be like, Wesley was so gentle with her. Wesley asked her if she had felt any different, he had heard that a woman after the first time feels different. Blossom thought; that was an odd thing to ask someone just after making passionate love together. Little did they know, but Blossom was now carrying what was the beginning of Wesley's child. Blossom didn't know then, but the first time for Blossom to make love and she gets pregnant. Blossom didn't know anything about love making except what she managed to read out of books. Before when she managed to get her hands on some books, Dawn would take them all away from her. Dawn wasn't able to bring herself to discuss those personal things with anyone, she would turn all blushed and walk away. After a couple of months had gone by from that evening in Wesley's loving arms, Blossom reached a point where her back side was getting much broader. Then one afternoon Dawn asked her, "Are You Pregnant Blossom?" That was a Saturday, but Blossom didn't think she was and answered back; quite shocked from the question, "No!"

In the next couple of weeks Blossom had realized that she had missed her monthly period in the last couple of months, Dawn had made a doctor's appointment for her to have a pregnancy test done.

Wesley had driven Blossom that Saturday afternoon to see the doctor. After what had seemed a long time waiting in the small filled waiting room to them. Blossom was then called into the examination room where she had to give a blood and urine sample before being examined.

Then came the most horrible part of all, Blossom was left in the examining room to change into one of those paper nities, you know the ones you can practically see through. When she had finished changing she was supplied with a paper blanket to put over her, while lying on the leatherette examining table. With all kinds of thoughts running through her mind of what was going to happen next while waiting for the doctor and nurse to come back in, in walked doctor Wade and a nurse. In the next scary moment Blossom was to find out what it was like for the first time to be examined how far along she was pregnant.

With in minutes Blossom was to find her legs to be placed and strapped into what they call stirrups, they look just like the stirrups on a saddle, only your legs are about two feet in the air while laying on your back.

Then they were spread apart about two feet wide, Blossom wasn't to have any panties on and the stirrups were made out of surgical steel, very cold on her bare skin. The set of two stirrups left her bottom wide open in the way she was placed in them. Doctor Wade preceded putting some kind of clear surgical gloves on and some cold metal clamp on her to hold open her vagina then entered his hand into her vagina. It was a frightening experience for Blossom.

For Doctor Wade; it was nothing; he had to feel if there was a baby's head forming in the womb. To someone who didn't know what to expect next, Blossom's most frightening fears came to life in the tests. Her rabbit had died, which meant that Blossom was now carrying Wesley's child for two months.

When Doctor Wade had finished examining Blossom he left the room and Blossom got changed back into her street clothes. Then he came back and gave her a lecture on getting pregnant before she was married. After the lecture was finished with Blossom, Blossom then went back into the waiting room and Wesley was called into the office for a lecture and chewing out.

On the way back home Wesley and Blossom were very quiet, until Blossom spoke out in anger and said bluntly, "I hope you are proud of yourself," She didn't mean to hurt Wesley's feelings, but she was scared that he might take off now and not marry her, even though they had been engaged for over two years now. In the Cartwright's family that was the wrong thing to have happen. You see Sheila was also pregnant before she was married, she was three months pregnant, now that Blossom was pregnant too it had almost broken Dawn's heart. In the same afternoon Blossom made her mother promise that she wouldn't tell Casey until after they were married.

Wesley's parent never knew that Blossom was carrying their grandchild until they were married for a couple of months. Blossom would hide the baby clothes in their large vanity drawer until it was time to tell them. The day Blossom and Wesley entered wedlock; it was the first day of snow, Blossom wanted to go to the church in a horse and buggy with a surrey on top, but it was too cold for that. The day of the wedding she wore a traditional full length gown of white lace and net over satin, with a shoulder length chapel veil and white floral head piece. Blossom carried a cascade of yellow rose buds and trailing variegated ivy.

They were married in the United Church on January the seventeenth. Blossom the daughter of Dawn and Casey Cartwright of Clover-Meadows exchanged vows with Wesley the son of Mr. and Mrs. Bailey also of Clover-Meadows, the Minister Attwood officiated at the double ring ceremony.

Coming down the isle on her father's right arm, Blossom looked radiant, as her gown swept over the artificial flowers that had been attached to the end of the pews the night before. Sheila had made them especially for the wedding by hand.

Leading the entourage were the maid of honor, Willette and the bridesmaid Cynthia, they wore floor length gowns of georgette and velvet in shocking pink which Dawn had sewn up for them; carried bouquets of pink sweetheart roses with chrysanthemums, in their hair they wore rose Buds. Dressed similar and carrying a nosegay of identical flowers was the tiny flower girl. Blossom's cousin Karen, ring bearer was Sheldon Williams.

Wesley's brother Roy was best man while friends of Wesley's, Gordon and a Chinese friend Ling, were both ushers. Organist was Mrs. O'Malley a neighbor friend of Wesley's. To received the many guests, Dawn choose a two-piece dress of off white and gold brocade; with off-white accessories. Her corsage was of yellow rose buds. Wesley's mother wore a dress of deep pink with rose color lace and a pink floppy hat. Her corsage was of white feathered carnations.

Master of ceremonies was an old friend of the Cartwright's family, Charley. The toast proposal was by Blossom's uncle Ralph Cartwright. For Blossom's going away outfit, she wore a dress and jacket of brown and gold foretell. Black paten shoes and accessories to match, a corsage of yellow roses. Out of town guests were Mr. and Mrs. Davidson of Victoria, Mr. and Mrs. Ralph Cartwright and family of Grand Bay. Wesley and Blossom resided in Clover-Meadows were Wesley was employed in building houses by Casey. The satin pillow their double rings were attached to was made by Dawn especially for Blossom's and Wesley's wedding ceremony. By snapping the rings on the satin pillow, that way Sheldon couldn't drop the rings while walking down the isle.

Wesley had gone out and bought a special two-piece black suit and white cotton dress shirt for his wedding. After the church services were over, the entire wedding party drove down to get their pictures taken at the Langdon studio. Poor Blossom she had to go to the bathroom; just as the photographer was ready to take pictures.

The washroom was so small that both she and her wedding gown were having a hard time to fit in there. Around five in the evening the wedding party finally arrived at the reception hall, the meals were served by the women from the legion committee, they were served hot roast beef dinner with all the trimmings.

While the dinner was being eaten, some of the guests usually the cousins of the bride, an old custom, started into tinkling their wine glasses with their forks or spoons, which meant that the bride and groom had to stand up and kiss, well! Every time Blossom and Wesley had started to take a bite of food they would tinkle their glasses. Poor Wesley, Blossom Thought that Wesley was rather enjoying the whole thing. That was all new to him being he was from a small family that had a hard time to make ends meet. Pretty soon everyone in the reception hall was tinkling their wine glasses. Blossom never did have a chance to finish her dinner, not that she was hungry, she was so much in love with Wesley; she couldn't care less if she had eaten or not.

When the time came that the dinner was finished the women from the legion came to clear away the dirty dishes, they brought out the three tired traditional wedding fruit cake that Dawn's girl friend made especially for the occasion. On each tier was four tiny clear wine glasses used as pillars. Then Wesley and Blossom would stand up behind their wedding table and have more pictures taken while cutting the cake together. When the cutting of the cake was finished the bride and groom plus wedding party including both sides of the parents would stand up in front of the wedding table to be congratulated on the wedding, more pictures were taken by individuals. Then after all the congratulation were done the music started to play, the first couple to dance a solo waltz was the bride and groom, which that music is usually picked out before hand by the bride and groom.

Then the wedding party would join in half way through the dance. While dancing with Wesley one of Wesley's old school chums recognize his car out front and came into say congratulation. He had spotted the two of them over in the far corner talking to Blossom's dearest girl friend, which she was two years younger than Blossom. The wedding reception lasted until midnight when Willette, Roy, Wesley and Blossom sneaked off quietly to get changed into their going away clothes. Willette was about to go up stairs at the Cartwright's home to Blossom's old bedroom with Blossom to help her out of her full floor length wedding gown, when Wesley spoke up and said, "I will help my wife now that we are married." Her wedding gown had quite a number of covered white buttons going down the back. You could hear Wesley and Blossom laughing quite a lot as Wesley struggled with the buttons.

By the time the four of them arrived back at the reception hall, the music stopped right in the middle of the dance and started playing "Here Comes The Bride", then Wesley escorted Blossom over to a wooden chair like the ones you would see in a bingo hall, for her to sit on, It was one of the guests that had placed the chair in the middle of the room, in which all the unattached gentlemen out in the audience gathered around while Wesley slowly proceeded to remove her homemade blue and white lace garter from just above her left knee. There in the middle of the dance floor Wesley threw the garter in the traditional way, meaning that he had his back to the gentleman and who so ever caught the garter was the next in line to be married. That was a very excited moment for all the unattached gentlemen.

One of the younger boys caught the blue garter as it went flying through the air towards his direction, he was only ten years old at the time. Since the young lad didn't know what to do with it, he gave it back to Blossom, Blossom still has that garter today. Blossom can still remember their wedding vows to this day; it went something like this she would say.

THE PEOPLE GATHERED HERE TODAY ARE HERE TO WHITENESS WESLEY BAILEY AND BLOSSOM CARTWRIGHT IN HOLY MATRIMONY, WE SHALL ALL KNEEL TO PRAY NOW.

This was the prayer as Blossom remembers it:

LOVE IS PATIENT AND KIND: LOVE IS NOT JEALOUS OR BOASTFUL: IT IS NOT ARROGANT OR RUDE. LOVE DOES NOT INSIST ON ITS OWN WAY: IT IS NOT IRRITABLE: IT DOES NOT REJOICE AT WRONG: BUT REJOICES IN THE RIGHT. LOVE BEARS ALL THINGS. BELIEVES ALL THINGS, HOPES ALL THINGS, AND ENDURES ALL THINGS. LOVE NEVER ENDS.

Then the Minister asked the people to stand and he said to Wesley: WILL YOU HAVE THIS WOMAN TO BE YOUR WIFE? Wesley answered. "I WILL." Then he turns to Blossom and asked her, "WILL YOU HAVE THIS MAN TO BE YOUR HUSBAND?" Blossom thought a moment and replied "I WILL." After that the Minister asked, "WHO GIVES THIS WOMEN TO BE MARRIED TO THIS MAN?" At that point Casey answered "I DO," then he took his place next to Dawn in the front pews. After Blossom handed her wedding bouquet to Willette, the maid of honor, to hold while they were holding hands. Wesley and Blossom joined hands as they looked at each other, Wesley repeated after the Minister.

IN THE PRESENCE OF GOD AND BEFORE THESE Witness," I WESLEY BAILEY TAKE YOU BLOSSOM CARTWRIGHT TO BE MY WIFE, TO HAVE AND TO HOLD FROM THIS DAY FORWARD, FOR BETTER, FOR WORSE, FOR RICHER, FOR POORER, IN SICKNESS AND IN HEALTH, IN JOY AND IN SORROW, TO LOVE AND TO CHERISH AND TO BE FAITHFUL TO YOU ALONE, AS LONG AS WE BOTH SHALL LIVE.

Wesley was finished saying his vows it was Blossom's turn to say her part now.

IN THE PRESENCE OF GOD AND BEFORE THESE WITNESS" I BLOSSOM CARTWRIGHT TAKE YOU WESLEY BAILEY TO BE MY HUSBAND, TO HAVE TO HOLD FROM THIS DAY FORWARD, FOR BETTER FOR WORSE, FOR RICHER, FOR POORER, IN SICKNESS AND IN HEALTH, FAITHFUL TO YOU ALONE, AS LONG AS WE BOTH SHALL LIVE.

At that point the rings were handed to the Minister from the satin pillow, in return he had handed the rings first to Wesley who placed the tiny band of gold on the third finger of Blossom's left hand and repeated after the Minister.

I GIVE YOU THIS RING THAT YOU MAY WEAR IT AS A SYMBOL OF THE VOWS WE HAVE MADE THIS DAY.

When the vows were finished being said, Minister Attwood spoke these words, "FOR AS MUCH AS WESLEY BAILEY AND BLOSSOM CARTWRIGHT HAVE MADE THIS SOLEMN CONVENT OF MARRIAGE BEFORE GOD AND THIS COMPANY, I DECLARE THEM TO BE HUSBAND AND WIFE. IN THE NAME OF THE FATHER AND THE SON, AND THE HOLY GHOST, YOU MAY KISS THE BRIDE.

That was a beautiful ceremony, Blossom remembered, she still has her wedding gown, veil, corsage and the blue garter the young fellow gave back to her. The corsage Blossom had pressed in the old Webster dictionary; they are now all put away in her cedar hope chest. After the reception was all over, around two a.m. Wesley and Blossom finally got to go on their honeymoon at the Red rooster Motel. By now they have turned that place into a lawn mower repair shop. The next morning the motel manager had swept the front walk off from the night snow fall. He also had sent up a free cup of tea and a donut to their motel room, Blossom was still fast asleep. That morning Blossom was a little bit home sick, so Wesley took her for a drive after breakfast around by her old neighborhood and up past her home, then out into the United States for a longer drive.

They only had a couple of days off work for their honeymoon; the both of them were due back bright and early Monday morning. Casey had hired Wesley prior to the wedding on his construction sight. Blossom was still working at the green house. They had found a quaint little basement suite which they rented the first three months. It was rather a funny place, there were no drawers for your cutlery in the kitchen, and when the people upstairs took a bath the shower down stairs would either be all hot or all cold water. There was only one bedroom and a small living room that was hardwood flooring. In that basement suite, Blossom had bought their first piece of furniture, a stereo with a blue tinted plastic lid. Wesley had picked the stereo out. That place was also were they bought their very first budgie bird, since they liked animals and fowls, but they were not allowed to have any other kind of four legged pet in that suite. When they had lived there for about three and half weeks, Blossom was having trouble sitting and having a bowl movement, she told Wesley how sore she was. Right away Wesley phoned Casey to say that he was taking Blossom to see the doctor. Which it turned out to be a really bad case of hemorrhoids, Blossom was to sit in a warm tub of water three times a day and put this ointment on when she came out, doctor wade had prescribed for her, since they only had a shower stall in their suite, Blossom had to be taken over to her parents every morning on the way home from work Wesley would swing by and pick her up. By the time that was all finished with, Blossom was getting further along in her pregnancy, it was getting time to look for another place to live, since there was no room for children in that suite. One evening Casey, Dawn, Wesley and Blossom all set out looking for another home; they found a little white and blue cottage on top of a hillside for rent. The cottage walkway roof was attached to the landlord's home next door, you had to go down a flight of stairs from the landlord's home to get to the cottage or you could drive in from the far side by the road. The landlord couple was about the same age as Wesley and Blossom.

In the cottage there were two bedrooms, both very small. The laundry room was in the bathroom which was across from one of the bedrooms. That living room and kitchen was as one combination with the furnace dividing the room off partly to one side. Blossom decided to divide the kitchen from the living room with their old gold color chesterfield; that Wesley's parents gave them when they got married. If you sat in the middle of that old chesterfield you would sink to the floor. The cottage was on an acre and hidden in behind some large ever green trees about a quarter of a mile off the road for privacy. The year was nineteen seventy when Wesley and Blossom had their first child, a little baby girl, she was born four in the morning on a sunny Monday. Blossom had a very easy time being her first child bearing experience. Since Blossom was always one for being well organized, before the dead line, they already had a name picked out for a baby girl, Wesley and Blossom decided on Bonny Jean.

Bonny Jean was a very pretty little girl weighing in at eight pounds seven ounces; she had a tiny blonde curl on the top of her head and the cutest pug nose. Bonny's eyes shone just like sapphires in the sunlight. She was born in the month July on the Twenty-Ninth day, it had rained all week before Bonny Jean was born, but Blossom managed to get a dozen quart bags of blueberries picked and ready for the freezer the evening before she went into hospital.

Bonny Jean arrived into this world that morning just as the sun decided to shine its brightest, then stayed shinning all day as if to say that here was being another special life entering into the world today. Around the hospital walkway all the flowers were out in their fullest bloom, the fragrance was a very sweet smelling aroma. After the nurses had finished cleaning up Blossom for the delivery room, Doctor Wade delivered little Bonny Jean. Doctor Wade then came back to the hallway behind the closed doors by the case room where the delivery took place, where they had Wheeled Blossom out on her hospital bed. Still feeling pretty weak, she managed to make a phone call to her parents who were anxiously waiting for the call to see what sex their new grandchild was.

Doctor Wade then asked Blossom if she would like to tell Wesley what sex the baby is, or if he should do the honors. Blossom being so excited about their first born wanted to be the one to tell Wesley first about their new baby. As doctor Wade was walking away down the corridor to visitors waiting room, just off to the right where Wesley was patiently waiting pacing up and down the floor, Wesley was wondering how Blossom and their new baby were doing, when doctor Wade walked into the room and congratulate him on the birth of their new child. Doctor Wade was puzzled for words as not to give the surprise of the sex of their child away, so he finally came out and said, "congratulation your wife just a had a Thing," poor Wesley being his first new born didn't know quite what to except, his face went three shades of white if there was such a shade. All the other expectant fathers in the waiting room thought he was going to faint right on the spot. Wesley had managed to pull himself together before seeing Blossom. She could see that something was bothering him, Blossom thought by telling Wesley the great news of his baby girl it would cheer him up, but it only made matters worse. She then asked Wesley to have a look in the nursery window where their little Bonny Jean was awaiting for her daddy to see her. When Wesley came back from the nursery, he had a very much proud type looks of a father on his face. Wesley wasn't standing there too long when his little Bonny Jean stuck her tiny tongue out at him, He had thought that it was funny for the very first time he seen his new daughter, she sticks her tongue out at him. Wesley thought it was so funny that he had almost forgotten everything doctor Wade told him; one hour prior, but when he had returned back to Blossom he remembered and told her all about it. Blossom just laughed, then said, "Doctor Wade was going to let me tell you the sex of our child, 'that was why he said it in that way to you." After having a little laugh they both felt much better that day. Blossom was in the hospital for about one week and every evening when it was visiting time, Wesley would be there beside her with their bundle of joy to hold.

That semi private room was filled with flowers and gifts for Bonny Jean and Blossom along with many congratulation cards. There wasn't much room for the other young girl's things, but she didn't mind and told Blossom so. When the day came that it was time for Wesley to come and take his new family home, they had one large special pink cardboard box from the hospital that was just filled with all the lovely gifts and cards, that box was to be used for Bonny Jean as a crib in case they didn't have one, but Blossom and Wesley had all ready one from Sheila's family and it was waiting for Bonny Jean at home.

By the time they had all arrived safely home, Blossom was pretty tired; she went to their bedroom for a rest, while Wesley was quite excited about having his new family home with him.

Then Wesley decided to put Bonny Jean down for her nap in her second hand crib, Sheila had given them the crib with three levels to put the mattress, as the baby grows you could put the base of the crib where the mattress lays so the child couldn't fall out. That crib use to belong to little Betty.

Little Bonny's bedroom was across from the bathroom, but next to their master bedroom. The first couple of nights being home, Blossom didn't hear Bonny crying the middle of the night, Wesley being a light sleeper would have to wake Blossom up in order for her breast feed Bonny.

Bonny's cry was quite soft for the first few months, then one evening they moved her into their bedroom in a bassinet that was loaned out to them by one of Blossom's Aunts. Even then sometimes Blossom still didn't hear little Bonny cry when she was hungry. It wasn't until Bonny was six months old that Blossom could hear her in the night. By then she was back in her own bedroom in the crib. When Bonny was couple of months old, Wesley and Blossom decided that they had spent enough time and money on Laundromats, so the three of them set out to buy a washer on a Saturday afternoon.

The Sears Department store had a sale on washers. While down looking at the washers, they ran into Casey and Dawn, Blossom had managed to save just so much money up towards a washer that was the price range they were going to have looked in. Dawn helped Blossom look at washers while Casey was busy talking to Wesley, they finally decided on a white Kenmore washer.

The cost was very small only two hundred dollars and fifty cents including tax. While they were shopping in the department store Blossom found the cutest little pink baby dress for Bonny, She had just enough money left over to buy it for Bonny.

Before Blossom had a washing machine she use to go to the Laundromat to do their basket loads of laundry, it was getting too expensive now, she would wash the laundry every day, since there were diapers to be washed every day now, Blossom would hang them outside on the clothes line just out back to dry.

In the winter the laundry would freeze dry on the line and Wesley's long pants would almost be able to walk in on their own, they were so stiff from the cold, Blossom would have to thaw them out in front of the furnace.

In the time to come Wesley would be apprenticing in construction with Casey building houses. They would do everything from digging the hole in the ground for the foundation to getting the carpets laid in the new home.

As time went by, Blossom would be expecting their second child, By that time they decided that little cottage was going to be too small for two children, they would have to start looking for another place to live. When; what seemed to Blossom as a long time they finally found another place to rent, but being the middle of the month, Wesley wasn't sure if they had to pay full months rent twice, one months rent for the cottage and one months rent plus half damage deposit for the new place.

The next morning Wesley went to see the landlord of the cottage who lived next door up a flight of stairs, he asked him if he found someone else to move in before the end of the month would they only have to pay half the months rent. The little cottage was up for sale anyway and Wesley figured sooner or later they were going to have to move. Wesley didn't figure that once it was sold that they would be able to stay anyway. You see by having someone else move in before the months end was up, they were able to save a half a months rent. The landlord of the cottage was in favor of the request, but it was only a verbal contract. Well! A couple of days later Blossom, Wesley and Bonny Jean had moved into their new farm house, Wesley had found a week prior. About a week later Wesley found a couple to rent the cottage. Only the old miserable landlord tried to say that there was no one moving in, even though Wesley had taken a drive by that afternoon and saw them moving in.

Those crooked landlords ended up taking Wesley and Blossom to court over that matter of the months rent. Blossom was about six months pregnant with their second child then. The people living in the cottage before Blossom and Wesley was the landlords sister and brother-in-law, in which they had written a letter stating that they had left the cottage in perfect condition before Wesley and Blossom moved in. What! a bunch of crooks, they had left the old harden bags of sugar in the bottom cupboard and the tile was coming up around the toilet. Blossom and Wesley had to clean the cottage from top to bottom before they could move in.

Wesley mentioned this to the judge while on the stand under oath in court, but unfortunately the judge was not about to listen to a young family man that day. Instead he listened to lying landlords who read a false letter the landlords' sister had written up that morning. The judge wasn't even going to listen to Blossom's father or her brother-in-law Grant as a witness.

In the end the landlord won the case and the judge wouldn't even listen to Wesley's testimony, they were sure glad to get away from that old landlord, actually he wasn't that much older that them, but he was sneaky as could be. Every Sunday morning he would start hammering above their bedroom window around six A.M., Most of the time he would wake Bonny Jean and not even give a darn.

One late afternoon while she was still pregnant with Bonny and while busy sewing on her quilt at the front hallway in front of the front door, only because there was no other place to put the sewing cabinet in the cottage. Wesley had come home from work with a silver toned wolf look like dog; that looked a lot like a wolf when it smiled at you, I think it was part shepherd." Blossom was so excited to have a dog that she nearly ran all the way out the door to hug Wesley.

The landlord was terrified of that dog and he use to stay far away from her as possible. Then Blossom went into hospital to have Bonny, Wesley took that dog to his Brother's to stay for awhile, at least until Blossom came back home from the hospital, but the dog ran away and never came back home again. You see they had her tied up in the truck, then put her in a wire cage pen that she didn't like too much. Blossom's dog was use to being in the house. That was the year they learned a lot about con-artist landlords and their false relatives

Chapter Nine

Getting a Helping Hand

The newly rented home for them was on five acre, the landlords were very nice grandparents, lived about one acre away separating the two homes. That farm style house was very large with two bedrooms off the huge living room, the kitchen off the spare third bedroom, an old furnace in the corner at the far end of the living room. The hot water tank was in the corner of the kitchen near the living room entrance. Off the kitchen was a small bathroom closes to the back door, outside the back door was a root cellar Blossom could put all her canning in. The floors, except the kitchen was all hardwood flooring.

Blossom had turned the third bedroom into a sewing room and a place to unpack her Tupperware every Monday afternoon, after returning home from the meeting at the warehouse. Then she would pack each individual order for her customers.

You see in the evening when Wesley was home with the Bonny, Blossom would go out to sell her Tupperware at home parties, which earlier in the week she had made the appointments. She did this to help put Wesley through carpentry school.

The course took four long years of struggling for them, and then one day Wesley would receive his journeymen papers. In the mean time he had a family to support. Blossom would save where ever she could and in the summer she did all her own canning then she would store them in the root cellar for the winter, the pump house was next to the root cellar, she was also able to store items in there too.

Blossom usually did about three hundred quarts of fruits and vegetables in a year. The back yard was large enough that they could have a huge vegetable garden. Wesley would help plant the peas, carrots, corn, sometimes even pop corn, lettuce, cucumbers, dill and pumpkins for selling at Halloween time, those would bring in littler extra cash, plus many more vegetables. The first time Blossom ever made a pumpkin pie, was the very first Halloween they lived together in the old farm house, she had kept all the guts from the pumpkin instead of the meats. Wesley had told her to keep the inside of the pumpkin, before he went. So that was what she did. They had a real good laugh over that one. That afternoon Wesley had gotten off work early, he had then shown Blossom which parts to use, after he laughed at it first. Wesley knew from many fresh pies his mother would bake ever Sunday Blossom and Wesley also had a black and white scruffy looking dog, he had one black marking covering over his right eye, and so they named him Patches. Patches use to go and play with the children in the school yard, every time the recess bell would ring that was his cue to go over there, until one afternoon Wesley was off work early and Patches was over in the school yard again just like so many times before playing with the children. Wesley caught him there and shocked the children by taking a pellet gun to his dog.

He knew when he shot the gun that it would only sting patches enough to make him stay home after that. There was no fear of Wesley missing and hitting the children, since he made the children move all out of the way first. The children thought that Wesley was crazy for shooting his own dog, but after that the children never coaxed Patches over to play again. Blossom was for ever chasing that darn dog out of her flower garden around the large fur tree, with the fur tree in the middle of her flower garden, it kept Blossom's head shaded during the hot afternoons when she was out there weeding in her beautiful flower garden.

Sometimes Mrs. Blair (the landlady) would even come over and help Blossom in her beautiful flower garden weeding; she always wore a large blue floppy sun hat to keep the sun from her frail face. Blossom didn't wear a hat; she hated wearing hats at any time. While she was still in her fifth month expecting their second child, Blossom would go out in her garden and weed, then Mrs. Blair would see her out in the garden and come over to see how she was doing, usually giving Blossom a helping hand. Mrs. Blair was a very friendly elderly lady, always warning Blossom not to do too much in her delicate condition. When they were finished in the garden Blossom would invite her in for a cup of tea and a fresh homemade biscuit with homemade strawberry jam. They would sit and chat for a while and then it would be time for Mrs. Blair to get supper started for her husband. Blossom and Mrs. Blair got along real well, thought Blossom as she went on to say how nice Mr. Blair was too, but Wesley and Blossom didn't see as much of him as they would of liked to. Mr. Blair had to go for long walks every day, usually in the evening for his heart, he had to exercise his heart by walking every day.

One day Wesley got together with some of their cousins and they loaded up Blossom's Uncle's half ton truck, Wesley was able to loan it for the afternoon, it was an old farm truck they loaded up with good potent chicken manure. Wesley had purchased this manure for a very low price, it was to help make the vegetable garden grow better. Boy! Was that ever well potent, Blossom would say as she was remembering the good old days.

Blossom would go on saying; it was so potent that you could have cured a cold with it. In that month the school was in progress which was directly next door to the left of the farm house. One of the children, "a little boy" thinks Blossom," shouted out real loud, Boy! That Stuff Stinks." The children played on the far side of the play grounds for the rest of that month.

About two months later in the middle of June on the eleventh day, Wesley had to rush Blossom to the hospital; she was admitted to the third floor of the Memorial hospital, that hospital was about ten miles from their home.

Close to two o'clock the very next morning, their second child was born to them, a bouncing baby Boy! With dark curly hair like the color of black coal at its shiniest and big blue eyes that could charm the pants off any women. They had picked the name Darcy. Which all ready had been picked out along time ago, if it was going to be a boy, they decided on Darcy. That was the time Wesley and Casey had put a one dollar bet onto see whether or not Wesley would be getting a son or a daughter for fathers day. Casey lost and to pay up in the hospital room.

Darcy was very sick in his first couple of days. He wouldn't breast feed or drink from a bottle for the first three days of his life. Blossom tried to breast feed him and that wasn't working, then she had to pump her milk out with a rubber pump made especially for women's breasts and the nurses would try to bottle feed him.

It was pretty painful and left her breasts quite sore for a couple of weeks, Blossom had to do that every morning and every afternoon until she was completely dried up inside.

Then the nurses would try to bottle feed Darcy again, nothing would work for him, yet he would scream his little lungs out so much that other patients at the end of the ward could hear him screaming.

Darcy wasn't a small baby, not by a long shot, in fact he weighed nine pounds fourteen ounces at birth. No if he was smaller baby the doctor told Blossom that he wouldn't have made it, as he had a very bad case of yellow jaundice.

There was this oriental nurse, she was much younger that the rest. one morning she came in while the two older English nurses were trying to help Blossom to get Darcy to breast feed, anyway this oriental nurse told Blossom in a very matter of a fact way that if you don't do something and feed that baby he is going to die. Well! That just put Blossom in a deeper depression than she all ready was in. In what seemed to be a couple of minutes later the oldest of the two English nurses went straight out into the corridor and gave that oriental nurse a piece of her mind.

That same afternoon Wesley came to visit with Bonny, Blossom was crying. Wesley just sat down beside her for awhile, after a few minutes had gone by he asked Blossom why she had been crying. Then the three of them walked down the corridor to the nursery window to see their Darcy. That's when Blossom told him what had happened earlier in the morning with the oriental nurse. Well! you should of seen the look on Wesley's face, he just marched straight over to the receptionist desk in the hall, between the nursery and Blossom's room, demanded that the oriental nurse was not to be near his wife and baby again.

By the time Darcy was a month old they decided to take a trip to the fruit country and visit some relatives. after just coming back from relaxing while fishing their car was just rolling around the steep hill, not far from her Aunt's home, Bonny was fast asleep on the pillows and blankets in the back seat with her seat belt on, Darcy was all strapped in his cuddle seat and then strapped in between Wesley's and Blossom's seat belts, which they were also wearing in their Toyota yellow car. Another car came speeding from behind and rear ended them, and then tried to get away with an almost flat tire, the children were a little shook up, but otherwise all right. Blossom was holding her own while Wesley could have cried out loud, their brand new car was only two months old.

There was a van with a couple of English people from out of state who had witnessed the whole accident when it happened. These people in the van had first gone to phone the police before coming back to see how Wesley's family was doing. Wesley and his family were standing by the side of the road in the middle of no where wondering what to do next. The police caught the Indian couple who had rear ended their car and charged them for leaving a seen of an accident, also for having no drivers license, the car had belonged to his Indian girl friend who fortunately had car insurance.

In the mean time while back by the road side the other police officer came and questioned Blossom and Wesley, then proceeded to question the nice English couple who had come back. It appeared that the Indian male driver was fooling around with his girl friend; and not watching where he was going. That English couple gave Wesley and his little family a lift to their relative's home. There they spent a couple of days while the car was being fixed enough to drive home again.

By the time Darcy was six months, things started to go all wrong with the hot water tank and the old pump in the pump house. Wesley being the type of guy who would rather fix things himself then to ask for any help, tried to fix the hot water tank the landlord came over about that time and caught him, in doing so he had to give Wesley and his family their notice.

So once again Blossom and Wesley had to go and find a place to stay in the one month's time. Blossom's parents had just purchased a parcel of land not far from where, Wesley and Blossom were staying. Casey offered the little white house for those few months to rent until Casey's own home was sold.

Blossom's parents had planned on tearing down the old shack and rebuilding a new Spanish house on the same spot.

It wasn't much of a house but it was a roof over their heads for the time being, they could have a dog, also there was enough room for a large vegetable garden again. So they all lived there for over a year. Then one day they found a sixteen year old house that had been up for sale on a quarter of an acre, since Blossom had managed to save a thousand dollars from the accident with the Indians, they had decided to talk it over with Casey, the three of them would go out and have a look at the house.

Blossom always liked to talk things over with her father; she respected his advice about matters in the importance. As her dad was a contractor of building houses on his own at the time, he had a pretty good idea on business such as theirs.

After having a good look at the place they all decided that it would be a pretty good buy for eighteen thousand-five hundred dollars, the very next day Casey, Wesley and Blossom all went to the lawyers to write up the agreement of contract while Grandma Cartwright was busy baby sitting Bonny and Darcy at her home.

The thousand dollars Blossom had saved went as a down payment on the house and Casey carried the montage being seventeen thousand-five hundred dollars, at a very low interest rate for them. It was then agreed that Wesley and Blossom would only have to pay Casey One hundred-forty dollars per month, which was including interest and principal in the agreement. So it was settled they had bought their very first home. The next day Wesley and Blossom had started packing up their belongings again as they were able to move in about one weeks time.

Chapter Ten

Owning Their First Home

The next three days and nights were to be spent cleaning up the old house. The elderly couple who lived in that house before hadn't bothered to so much as clean it out before they had left, in fact they just ate and left with their car and utility trailer packed with as much as they could squeeze into it for their travels to the one hundred mile house.

There was cupboards filled with food and dishes that hadn't been cleaned out, some of the dishes were cracked and some had hardly been used, in actual fact they had even left the butter dish with the butter still in it and a knife that had been used sitting on the counter top by the stove.

Wesley figured maybe they weren't moved all the way out as of yet, so he phoned the Realtor to see what the scoop was on the house, while talking to the Realtor he had found out they had left early that morning for the one hundred mile house.

At the front of the little white and blue house at the far end was a bedroom filled with their belongings. That was to be the master bedroom; it was the biggest of the three. There was still a single bed and mattress plus clothing thrown on the bed and all over the floor, even some clothes still hanging in the closet. In one of the closets there was a small brown cardboard box that hadn't even been opened, so Blossom with her curiosity opened the box quickly, having been left behind with the rest of the belongings they found a brand new olive green four piece coffee set in the box. Well! neither one of them drank coffee, so it was to be put aside for a Christmas present since all their money had gone into the little house they hadn't had too much for Christmas this year. Wesley's sister Amy and her husband drank coffee so that was to be a perfect gift for them. On the fourth day they had brought Darcy and Bonny along with them cleaning up the old house once again, but Blossom found that she was doing more running around after the two children then she was cleaning.

So the next day Grandma and Grandpa Cartwright looked after the children until ten o'clock that evening. When Blossom was starting to find herself getting sleepy, Wesley decided after finishing some of the painting in the living room that was enough work for them tonight, they still had to pick up Darcy and Bonny and have a good night sleep, then they could have a fresh start in the morning again.

Grandma had fed the children and was just about to relax in front of the TV, while Darcy and Bonny were fast asleep in Grandpa's bed up stairs, then Blossom and Wesley arrived to take their sleeping children home. While sitting around chatting in the large living room, Dawn decided to serve some tea and biscuits, then it was time to take the children home.

Being a Saturday they started out again the very next morning after dropping the children off at their Grandparents home again. While Blossom was busy cleaning out the kitchen cupboards, Wesley was out back helping Minister Thomas loaded up his station wagon and utility trailer, with the articles that were left behind for the church bazaar sale coming up.

There was such things like clothing men's and women's, dishes that weren't cracked too badly, some food such as spices etc. lamps and antiques, even the single bed and mattress went to the church, all for the sale that was to take place in the basement church on the following Sunday.

Wesley wasn't a steady attendant at church even though Blossom would of liked him to be, but he did believe in the church and he did always help out the church when ever he was able to.

The food that Blossom thought might not be very good, she discarded out in the large garbage bags at the back door. The other food she either kept herself which was very little or gave it to the church as a donation where they had both their children Christened in. There was this one pair of old but good leather men's boots that was too small for Wesley in the third small bedroom closet.

This elderly man who didn't have too much and was crippled some what lived in the old remodeled chicken coop just in behind them, came over to see his new neighbors. That was when Wesley gave him the boots. "Well! You never saw a more appreciative man in all your born days, than he was for those second hand pair of old leather boots.

The next day and night were spent cleaning and painting that old run down house, while Grandma and Grandpa had their hand full with Bonny and Darcy. Blossom and Wesley washed ever wall and floor in that place, those bathroom walls looked as though the people before them had taken their dirty water and literally threw it all over the walls, "they were just black with dirt." When Blossom started to wash the bathroom walls just around the tip of the tub she had discovered that the walls were actually apricot in color, it showed how dirty those walls really were, "Blossom would say with a vexed tone in her voice.

As she was washing down the bathroom walls, Wesley was busy scrubbing the turquoise green tiling on the kitchen floor; the kitchen was the largest room in the house. Those floors had to have a steel brush taken to them in order to make those floors come clean again. Where the fridge and stove use to be was a large black ring of grease that was next to the bottom cupboards.

In the living room they had an old blackish grey indoor-outdoor carpet nailed to the beautiful hardwood floors, "Now! did you ever hear of such a ridiculous thing to do in all your born days," Blossom would say, This was also done in the bedrooms and the hallway that ran into the kitchen, both the hallway and the kitchen were painted a deep royal blue.

In the morning you could turn on the over head kitchen light and not even know that the light was on. The living room was painted a pale green with light pink trim on the valance, around the edge of the ceiling was also painted pink. Wesley quickly changed the color to an off white before they ever moved in. By the time Wesley and his family finally moved in the house it was all cleaned up and the living room was finished being painted.

On the east wall in the living room was a huge old fashioned fire place with a wooden mantel in a rust color. The following week was to be doing projects in which they would be purchasing the color of paint for the kitchen and hallway. It was to be a bright yellow in the kitchen and shinny off white in the hallway.

That was going to cost a lot of money that they just didn't have at the time, so Blossom got up more Tupperware parties in the evening in order to buy the paint they needed.

Blossom was thinking then about just how lucky she was not to have that petit-mal anymore, or she wouldn't have been able to do the things she can do today. Yes! Blossom and Wesley had a lot of fixing up to do in the old house before it was just right, since both didn't mind the hard work that was laid ahead of them, they both enjoyed the challenge.

Outside their home was a beautiful huge purple lilac bush, just on the left side as you drive on the gravel driveway that led into the single garage. Under their bedroom window was about three or four bushy shrubs that needed attending to fairly quickly. That was to be Blossom's job, since she didn't mind puttering around in the garden. Wesley was at his job sight when the first set of company came over to visit. He was still in construction work, working for Casey.

The shrubs needed pruning and the trees around the ditch in the front yard needed to be weeded out and trimmed too. Their yard was a quarter of an acre, in the back yard there was a huge old oak tree the children persisted to climb, it was located in the middle of the unfenced back yard.

In the summer months Blossom would put out the children's wadding pool out front in the yard and in they would jump splashing each other. Bonny loved the water she was like a fish in the water. When she was to get her bathing suit all wet, the very first thing she would do was to strip off the wet bathing suit, no matter who was watching her at the time.

It took Blossom many months to be able to teach her that a bathing suit was meant to get wet. Some days she would even take her brother's trunks off and then down the road they would streak before Blossom would have a chance to catch them. Bonny was about three and Darcy was about two years at the time There was this one day that Darcy thought he was doing his daddy a favor early in the morning, he had stuck the garden hose down the exhaust pipe of Wesley's motorcycle, then filled the exhaust pipe with water. After that the bike didn't work too well.

There was this young fellow who wanted to buy the bike for joy riding, Wesley use to use the bike to go back and forth to work in the summer as the car was too expensive on gas to run every day. Blossom didn't mind him selling the bike; she really thought that the bike was too dangerous anyway.

As Blossom was cleaning out some packing boxes one afternoon, she came across some old love letters that they had written to each other many years prior to their wedding day.

There was this one love letter that Wesley had written to her while he was working out of town for his Grandfather. That letter was written on stationary that had candy kisses for sale in an old bucket and verse that read:
SINCE YOU'VE BEEN GONE I'VE BEEN SAVING ALL MY KISSES JUST FOR YOU. Then he wrote I MISS YOU SO, AND AS YOU CAN SEE I HAVE BEEN SAVING ALL MY KISSES JUST FOR YOU. Wesley often joked about that sort of thing, He always wrote her when he was away, they weren't real mushy letters, just letters to let Blossom know what he had been doing with his time and how much he had missed her.

Blossom would spend hours going through the old love letters she had saved. This would be when Bonny and Darcy were fast asleep and Wesley was busy at work, it was Blossom's quiet time.

Some days after she had put the children down for their afternoon nap, Blossom would clear up the kitchen, then go and relax by herself as she would get these terrible mind splitting migraine headaches. Blossom said, "ever since she out grew her petit-mal she had gotten those terrible headaches, she believes at the time she had thought that God had exchanged her Petit-mal for the headaches. The only way to get rid of them was to have a sleep with a cold cloth or ice bag on her forehead in a dark room where it was quiet, some days that didn't even help, if Blossom took aspirin she would get sick to her stomach. A lot of times it would be so intensive that she would wish she could take her head off of her shoulders for the evening. Some nights when her headaches would come, they would stop her from enjoying a good night of love making.

Poor Wesley he didn't know what to do for her headaches. When Blossom would have those migraine headaches, she would sometimes get up set with the children for making so much noise, she would never hurt the children, and she might just send them to their room to play though.

Every Monday after the Tupperware meeting was finished in town. Mrs. Bailey would give Blossom a ride home in her station wagon, but Blossom couldn't enjoy the meeting or the ride home, she usually got those migraine headaches halfway through the meeting. Then on the way home she would start to feel car sick, Blossom got car sick on long trips. Blossom did do fairly well in selling the Tupperware and she would receive some pins with rhinestones mounted in the number of sales she made for the week. Blossom wasn't the highest seller but she did not bad, she would say. Sometimes Blossom's headaches would last three days straight, but she was glad that it wasn't her petit-mal. At least she knew what she was doing when she had a migraine headache. Not like when she use to black out and make a fool of her self.

While Blossom was thinking about her past, she found another letter that was written when she was up visiting her sister Sheila on the little Island. Blossom remembered that the mail was on strike at the time she had written Wesley, he had written her a letter which turned out to be dated the same day as her letter, Boy! Great minds sure do think alike.

As Blossom read the letter she could feel another one of those migraine headaches coming on, she was glad that the children were fast asleep tucked in their beds this time, at least she would have peace and quiet for awhile before they wake.

In the letter she was reading at the time from Wesley, it stated that he was putting up siding and wished that she was there with him. Then she came across a letter she had wrote back to him, Blossom mentioned to Wesley that when she gets back home she will be helping her mom pick strawberries again. At that time Blossom was hired part time in the strawberry field as she was still working full time at the green house.

Blossom read further and came across the time she was applying for a job in Clover Meadows office, she had wrote in the letter, "YOU KNOW HOW IT IS WHEN YOU HAVE PETIT-MAL, NO ONE WANTS TO TOUCH YOU," THEY MAKE YOU FEEL LIKE SOME SORT OF A FREAK. The only way Blossom got her job at the green house was by not telling them about her petit-mal until they had judged her fairly by her work not by her illness.

As Blossom was reminiscing the good old days, Wesley walked in through the bedroom door; she had been sitting with her back to the door on their seventy-five year old cherry wood double bed. That bedroom suite use to belong to one of Wesley's neighbors that let them buy it fairly cheep for their very first home, the whole five piece bedroom suite only cost them forty-five dollars.

Wesley startled Blossom just then, she told him what she was doing when he startled her, Wesley had thought she had been silly reading those old love letters, then he bent down and kissed her forehead very gently. They both had a good chuckle reading old love letters after that.

Wesley had found this one letter from Blossom's parents written on a back of a paper place mat from one of the restaurant they were in, it read:

WELL! HOW GOES THE BATTLE, Blossom's dad always started out a letter in that manner, WE ARRIVED AT SHEILA'S AND GRANT'S JUST IN TIME FOR A DELICIOUS SUPPER. HAD A BIT OF A WAIT AT PR. ROBERTS FROM ONE-FIFTEEN TO FOUR-THIRTY, BUT ALL MANAGED TO GET ON THE SAME PLANE. IT WAS CALLED A GOOSE, TOOK OFF IN THE WATER, BUT LANDED ON DRY LAND A VERY SMOOTH FLIGHT. ALL ARE FINE; BETTY HAD GROWN A LOT AND HAS A PONY TAIL NOW.

At that point Blossom couldn't read any more as she was having a hard time to hold back the tears that were wailing up in inside her, since it wasn't too long ago that Betty had passed away from the ones who loved her so, She had leukemia. Blossom was very close to Betty in her short time on earth. So Wesley looked through the old cardboard box that they kept all their old letters in, to try and see what other kind of letters he could find to try and cheer her up.

As he never knew what to do when Blossom would start her crying, like most men Wesley felt helpless around a women that cried.

Blossom was very sensitive, more so than most people knew, she cried over most sentimental things, but there was no other love letters to read. Wesley just walked out the bedroom and left her to be by her self for awhile.

He played with Bonny and Darcy in the living room as they didn't have a basement in that old house. Wesley knew that Blossom wouldn't be crying too long, because even though she couldn't help herself from crying sometimes, she felt that it was silly to cry over things you can not change. Soon she would be joining them and they would be laughing again.

Chapter Eleven

Their Trip to Hawaii

 The very next day, Blossom was making lunch for Bonny and Darcy while Wesley was out earning a living for his family; he was big on responsibilities now. Blossom heard on the radio station about a contest that you could win free groceries in the mater of a few minutes of shopping at a particular grocery store in that shopping centre. If your name was picked, the grand prize was a trip for two to Hawaii. All you had to do was send a certain box top with your name, address and telephone number to the radio station by a certain time limit.
 Blossom was always sending a different box top on all kinds of contests to try and win this or that. First she searched all the cupboards for the products they had mentioned, then when she found the ones she was looking for she sat down and wrote her name, address and telephone number on a four by four inch sheet of paper, that was the usual requirements for the contests and stuffed it in along slender envelope with the box tops, mailed it to the radio station that very same afternoon.
 The very next box top she sent in was from a potato chip box, Blossom would send in some every week until the contest was all over, but she never did win any free groceries. Then one sunny afternoon in the month of August while her neighbor friend was over having tea and chatting at the large kitchen table, the children were fast asleep. The phone rang; it was a wall phone above the kitchen table, and Blossom answered the phone in her usual friendly voice, thinking it was her Mother, Dawn often phoned up just to have a chat and see how things were going with them. Hi! Blossom would say, Hi! Instead of Hello, Her family use to laugh about the way she would answer the phone, but Blossom learned along time ago in selling Tupperware that it makes you smile and vibrations will be felt on the other end, when you say Hello, it makes you sound like you

are frowning. Anyway back to the phone call, it was the radio station that had the contest going, who was on the phone. Blossom had thought that it was all over and she had for gotten all about the grand prize.

As Blossom was listening, she couldn't believe what she actually was hearing coming from the man on the other end, he was taping the conversation he told her, then said: "IF YOU CAN ANSWER THIS SKILL TESTING QUESTION CORRECT, YOU WILL HAVE WON A TRIP FOR TWO TO HAWAII. "So Blossom not believing what she had just heard answered the question correctly, the question was: WHICH RIVER RUNS THROUGH THE FRASER VALLEY?" Of course everyone knew it was the Fraser River.

As Blossom hang up the phone she told her girl friend Connie about the phone call, but Connie didn't believe it and decided to go home, so she wouldn't spoil Blossom's dream. On the way home Connie was thinking, poor Blossom falling for a gag like that one," Blossom had just gone to sit down in the living room on the old worn out couch to collect her thoughts, she was thinking maybe it was a gag, there was a lot of that going on just then, when suddenly the phone rang again, she still was in a bit of a daze from the first call, this time it was a lady's voice on the other end from the radio station, she was calling back to confirm the earlier call, since Blossom sounded on the phone like she hadn't believed it The Lady wanted Blossom to be sure that she knew that the earlier phone call was on the level, and not one of those prank calls that was going around then.

Blossom got so excited then, something she was never aloud to do before, but now that she was no longer with petit-mal hanging over her, she felt like yelling on the top of the mountain to everyone down below she had won a trip for two to Hawaii. Right away Blossom phoned her mother and cousin to tell them the good news and to be sure that they would listen to the radio station for the recording. It turned out that one of her cousins was all ready in Hawaii and that he would still be there when Wesley and Blossom arrived in December.

Blossom then had a brain wave to phone the work shed on the construction site where Wesley was working, building houses, he wasn't working for Casey anymore. His boss answered with a firm but boss like manner. Blossom knew Wesley didn't like to be bothered at work, but this time was something that couldn't wait until he had gotten home that evening, so Blossom just told the boss who was very nice to pass the message onto Wesley she would be so grateful. After Blossom had finished telling her whole story about the trip to Wesley's boss. "I'm sure he wouldn't n mind being bothered for something like that," He told Blossom. Blossom asked if they could listen to the radio station right away, as they had been playing back the taped conversation on the air.

That evening when Wesley finally arrived home he had told her what all happened at work after her phone call, apparently one of the workers had a radio in his car, they all gathered around to listen to the announcer, as they were all gathered around the car listening very carefully, Wesley heard the announcer say; "AND THE WINNER OF THE GRAND PRIZE, A TRIP FOR TWO TO HAWAII WAS MRS. BLOSSOM BAILEY."

Wesley said, at first he didn't believe it, then said to the co-worker after he had heard Blossom's voice on the radio. "SON OF A BITCH SHE DID DO IT." The fellow co-workers were very happy for Wesley and they all congratulated him, by that time there was only maybe an hour or so left of work for the day anyway. On the way home he dropped off at the Cartwright's to tell them the good news, but Blossom had all ready beat him to it.

Wesley was grin from ear to ear that evening. In the next couple of months they were spent getting ready for the trip. They had to go to the radio station and receive the plane tickets and, reservations had to be made months ahead of time, also they got their pictures taken; receiving an empty envelope to look like the real thing the tickets weren't in as of yet, so Blossom had to settle for the empty envelope for the picture. The pictures were for the local news paper to go into the next week's issue. When the local news paper came out with their story in it; it read:

TWO WEEKS HAWAII HOLIDAY FOR TWO WAS WON BY BLOSSOM AND WESLEY BAILEY, IN A DRAW CONDUCTED BY EIGHT SUPER GROCERY STORES AND THE RADIO STATION. More than 2,600 ENTERERS WERE MADE IN THE SHOPPING SPREE CONTEST. ARRANGEMENTS FOR FUN TRIPS FOR MR. AND MRS. BAILEY ARE BEING MADE FOR THE END OF DECEMBER BY WAYNE THE MANAGER OF THE TRAVEL SERVICES.

The pictures were in black and white and Blossom kept a copy of it, as well as most of their relatives. Come December Wesley and Blossom were all ready for their trip to Hawaii, they had made arrangements for the children to stay with their grandparents. Casey and Dawn gave them one hundred dollars to share and spend how they liked to in Hawaii.

Since the Cartwright's had given them some money, Wesley's parents felt that they should too, Blossom and Wesley felt bad because the Bailey's were not well off, but they insisted on giving twenty dollars, Mr. Bailey slipped a twenty dollar bill into Wesley's hand the night before the flight. When the time came to catch the plane, they managed to scrape up four hundred dollars between the two of them for spending money. It wasn't too much money to take to a place like Hawaii to have a really good time, but in those days that was a lot of money for Wesley and Blossom. Casey drove them down to catch the plane, all the way down to the airport Casey was teasing Wesley that he was going to go in his place and Blossom was teasing right along side her father, she would say things like he had more money to spend on her and that she would take him along just for his money.

The roads were very icy; they had to take it very slow so the only person who came to see Blossom and Wesley off was Casey. Blossom was getting worried that they might miss the plane by now. Finally arrived at the airport safely and was checked in for their flight, said their good-by's and thanked Casey, went up the ramp towards the 707 jet plane, there they were presented with a blue and white flight bag to take on with them and keep.

As Blossom and Wesley entered the airplane they were seated in certain seats that were numbered for the rest of the flight. Blossom was seated in the middle of three seats across in a row. Wesley was by the window and another elderly lady on the isle side, the seats had high backs and arms rests between each seat. There seats were located halfway down the plane on the right hand side, above them were luggage racks you could put your heavy coats and camera cases in, in front of you attached to the back of the seat were trays that you could pull out for meals, beneath the trays was a pocket liked you would find in a car filled up with magazines and a brown paper bag to be sick in if you needed it. Wesley had all ready seated himself down when the elderly lady had spoken to him, since they couldn't talk with Blossom between them, she and Wesley exchanged seats and Blossom was now by the window looking down as the plane took off. Blossom didn't mind that she liked the window seats better anyway.

As she was looking out the window seeing all the people in the cold snow, Blossom was thinking how lucky they were to be going to Hawaii this time of the year. Wesley was only on one other airplane in his early years and that was when he was in the air force training. They left Canada at nine A.M. with 60 above outside, very cold thought Blossom. After the plane had taken off she heard the pilot come on the loud speaker, this is a 707 jet you are now flying in at 50 mph at 35, 000 feet in the air.

Just after they took off they were served a good lunch, Blossom noticed there were severities placed in individual serviette holders made of plastic with the flight name on them. She figured they were for souvenirs, so Blossom put one in her purse for keep sake from the trip. The passengers were also served alcohol drinks with their meals if they wanted, that was something different, "thought Blossom, as she put a spoonful of salad to her mouth and drank a bit of mai tai that was ordered earlier for her.

The plane arrived in Hawaii at 2:05 P.M. coming in the wind was bit choppy, it was 65 degrees in the plane so by the time they had finally arrived, most of the people had taken off their outer coats and sweaters, but Blossom and Wesley had only brought summer clothing. They were told ahead of time that it was going to be very hot in Hawaii. At first the passengers were picked up by a long black coach that took them over to the terminal to pick up their suitcases. Which the workers had managed to put Blossom's large Tupperware suitcase on the bottom, the weight of the other suitcases broke the sides of it, it was a large heavy one that was right on top of hers. Blossom had to take it to be fixed before returning back home. As they went through customs, Blossom was thinking, "I sure hope they don't wreck the hair setter Wesley gave me for Christmas two years ago." Soon they were greeted in the tradition Hawaiian style with leis and kisses on the cheeks. The very next day they were all taken to a free breakfast, a band was playing Hawaiian music, lots of fruit and coconut to eat, it was a smorgasbord breakfast in one of the larger hotel dinning areas, the room was just packed with people when Blossom and Wesley had finally arrived. Blossom noticed the name of the Hotel they were staying in was called the Sand Castle. On the third day the two of them spent getting up early, then did more shopping and sight seeing, only this time it was for the relatives back home they had shopped for. Wesley also bought a few greeting cards to send to Bonny and Darcy. On their free time from the tour they went shopping and more shopping; some of the native stores had air conditioning which felt very cold to Wesley and Blossom, they came in from the hot sunshine to find the air conditioning very cold on their bare skin. As they walked along the beach that afternoon kicking the sand between their bare feet just taking in the warmth of the day, by the time they started to feel tired from all the walking and warm sunshine, they headed back to the Hotel room, but on the way back Blossom found this little market place and they found themselves going through the market place looking at all the neat gifts that was there. Wesley and Blossom arrived back at their Hotel room around twelve midnight and very tired from the long walk in the sunshine.

    After awhile Wesley took Blossom driving to see the rest of the Island. Blossom and Wesley arrived back at their hotel room about nine thirty P.M. That evening they had a short rest and then up again to see a singer at the Polynesian palace.

    The tickets some lady dressed up like a mermaid gave them earlier in the market place, Blossom said it only cost them three dollars each instead of twenty-five dollars each. Those tickets paid for the entrance fee, the only thing they had to pay for was their drinks. If you had bought a double drink, the first one was free; no matter if it was liquor or a soda drink, it all cost the same in that small crowded entertainment lounge. Blossom remembers how smoky it was in the dim lit room, but she said the stage where the singer was very well lit. Don (the singer) would ask "Is there any Birthdays, or anniversaries in the house tonight"? Blossom and Wesley's third Anniversary had just celebrated two days prior to the day of the concert; Wesley didn't feel it was right for them to say they were celebrating their anniversary since it wasn't on that day. Wesley later was glad that he didn't say they were celebrating their anniversary, or they would of had to go on stage and act like a fool too. When the program was all over Blossom bought one of his records, then everyone lined up in the crowded back room where he was busy signing the record albums. Don would write on the cover what you asked him to, since Blossom couldn't think fast enough what he could write for her, he just said, "To Blossom from Don.

The next morning Blossom and Wesley were up at the crack of dawn, got dressed in something very cool, then set out for a drive to the navy base where they had a tour through the pearl harbor memorial ship, it was built in the middle of the ocean, that memorial was built right over the ship that had gone down in the pearl harbor attack. On the dock was some little shops in which you could purchase items of the pearl harbour for keep sakes. They went into the little shop after their tour and saw what they had to offer. Wesley found this one record in which it had the whole story of the pearl harbor attack on, even the swishing of the waves against the ship.

By twelve noon they had brought the sports car back to the rental agent. There was this little café along the beach that Wesley and Blossom stopped off on the way to their hotel room, the food was out of this world, very inexpensive too. That sunny afternoon was just too hot for anyone to be walking along the beaches; in fact she noticed that they were very few people out walking any place just then.

On the fourth day of their vacation they got up later than usual and went down to the shopping centre, where Wesley bought a bathing suit for Blossom, she tried on many different ones, finally settled for the one piece suit, it was a pink and white floral with a low cut back, Blossom had tried on some bikinis, but with her figure they made her look like she was only wearing a handkerchief on top and bottom. That bathing suit made Blossom look very attractive with her long blonde hair trailing past her shoulders. Now don't get the wrong idea, Blossom would say," I sure wasn't any beauty queen or anything that pretty," I was I guess you would say average looking." The only thing I had going for me was my long blonde hair," Blossom went on to say, the one piece bathing suit Wesley picked out cost twenty-five dollars American, she felt bad about him spending so much money on her when they didn't have much to spend in the first place. After purchasing the bathing suit they hurried back to the hotel room to get changed into their bathing suits to be ready by ten A.M. for the bus to pick them all up outside their hotel to go to the private beach party, it was a Bar-B-Q beach party put on by the Hawaiians especially for the ones on the tour. For the beach party the tour guide had hired a live band to play for them, the band was all dressed in Hawaiian costumes. The water was so warm and clear that sunny afternoon, Blossom remembers," thinking just how clear the water was, but she soon found out that is also was very salty when she caught a mouthful of water from one of the bigger waves. The waves were very large out there and they would come swishing up against their lily white bodies while standing in the water to cool down. After their warm swim they all were treated out for a huge lunch Hawaiian style, then bathed in the warmth of the sunshine while listening to music on the sandy beach. The waves washing up against the rocks on shore; all in all it was a very enjoyable afternoon. When some of the people had enough of laying around lapping up the sun, they would get up and dance in the sand to the soft glowing music, with sand beneath their feet feeling very warm and soft squishing between their toes. Blossom remembers how romantic it felt back then. By four that afternoon the beach party was finished and all had to get their towels and what ever else they had brought to the party then climb back into the bus headed back to the hotels.

Blossom washed out their swim suits in the hotel bathroom sink so that the salt water wouldn't ruin them, and then hung them to dry on the shower rod over night. After that she washed the salt water out of her hair so the salt not do damage her blonde hair, by the time they were ready for sleep, Blossom's hair was all dry again.

The warm air was too hot still to get any proper sleep that night; instead they just decided to sit up talking most of the evening.

On the fifth day they went out to the Kodak show, since it wasn't too far from the hotel they walked. Wesley and Blossom walked along the lagoon and through the zoo hand in hand over to where the Kodak show was playing.

At the show there was one occasion where a native boy who was climbing a palm tree to the top and back down the huge tree again without any climbing gear. Blossom thought that was really something to see, but Wesley had his eyes on the Hula girls dancing down bottom from the bleachers they were sitting in, a typical man thought Blossom as she smiled at her husband.

The way back to the hotel room was spent stopping at the zoo to watch some of the animals, and then back to the market place. Often they would just walk through just to look at the different carvings. At about one-thirty in the hot afternoon they decided to rent a small sports car for a twenty-four hour period, went driving around the Island side. Blossom thought it was so romantic just the two of them, they stopped at Blow Hole where they looked at all the pretty scenery, then sugar cane fields, Wesley and Blossom walked the rest of the way through the fields, along the way Blossom stooped down to pick up a sugar cane that had been lying on the ground broken off. She thought she would be able to take it back home to show the children where sugar came from, but Wesley told her she had better just leave it there The very next stop was through the pine apple fields and onto the culture place where Blossom found some coconuts left lying about on the ground, the grounds men had been busy trimming the coconut trees. Blossom asked if she may have that one coconut that was still green on the outer shell; the men smiled and gave it to her. They were back to the hotel just in time for supper, went down to the little store on the ground floor of the hotel to see what they could find for supper while in their room that evening.

Wesley and Blossom's money was starting to run out, Wesley started to talk to one of the cab drivers that use to live in Canada as he had found out later. It turned out that his name was Victor and he worked out of Charley's place, Victor had come over to Hawaii about ten years prior. At that point he offered Wesley and Blossom to ride free in his taxi around the Island that evening.

Now they were very surprised that Victor had offered a free tour and a bit surprised of the free taxi trip. "I mean well! Who would offer anything free now days without any strings attached? Victor told them to talk it over by themselves while he waited for their decision, finally they decided to take him up on his generous offer, Wesley had said to Blossom, "what's there to loose," so off they went with Victor, a very nice elderly man, but they were worried that he might leave them some place stranded if he got another call. Victor gave them fifteen minutes to go upstairs in their hotel and get a sweater on, as the night air was rather chilly. The very first stop was to Diamond Head mountain, it was so beautiful thought Blossom in the moonlit evening with all the lovers walking around hand in hand, Victor pointed out the different points of interest, after leaving them along on Diamond Head for awhile he then took them up to the Milton hotel where some of the movie stars stayed. In one end of the hotel there was a lagoon where the stars could take a swim or just lay around in the water, then on the other side of the same hotel there was another lagoon where they kept the Bawana fish etc. The chandelier Blossom remembers thinking how huge it was and it looked as though the chandelier was made out of heavy rice paper, a clear sort of paper that you could enjoy the full enchanting view of the lights. After the hotel, Victor took them through the university grounds and onto the court yard, where there he pointed out the huge ban yon trees that took up an acre of its own. At the state capital building there was a royal palace, it was built in china town, then they went through the heart of the slum area, this was when Victor had told them to be sure that their doors and windows were locked and closed tightly, Blossom knew why when saw a fellow dressed up like a women with lipstick and the whole ladies of the evening outfit on.

From there they went off to another top of the mountain, it was so beautiful, remembered Blossom as she spoke of what it was like to be left alone on the top of that mountain with her sweet Wesley, while Victor waited patiently in his cab for them. Blossom remembers then that they really couldn't enjoy the full romantic evening on that night that Victor had so carefully provided for them, they were always afraid of being left stranded, since he had told them he had to put his meter on at the beginning even though he wasn't going to charge them. You see they kept expecting Victor to take off without them, the two of them were afraid they wouldn't know their way back to the hotel if that occurred or even worse maybe at the end of the tour they would have to pay for the whole trip, and it was up to twenty-five dollars American currency. By now their imagination was going wild.

After seeing the King Kamahi statue, Victor then drove them back to the hotel that Wesley and Blossom were staying at, he just said, "Now all I want you two to do is go up stairs to bed and have a good night sleep. Blossom couldn't believe her ears what they were hearing on that wonderful evening. She quickly got her camera and took a picture of him standing by his cab. Wesley didn't say too much, but was shocked at the generosity too of this stranger. Since it had turned out to be a thirty dollar taxi trip and they didn't have to spend a penny on it. Blossom figured that to the family back home to believe them she had better have a picture to prove this.

Victor was very nice and the only reason he did it was, he figured that if you do something nice for someone, then they will do something nice for you, by telling people about the taxi driver and the tour they had.

January the twelfth which was the very next day, they managed to sleep in late that morning even though the sun was out bright, in Hawaii it's usually too hot to sleep in late, but that morning it turned out to be a little cooler than the days prior. When Blossom and Wesley finally did wake up they got dressed fast and went straight down stairs to buy some hard boiled eggs, a loaf of bread and a jar of jam for their breakfast, they weren't suppose to eat meals in their hotel room, but they were fast running out of money and needed to cut down somewhere before their holiday was over, besides they weren't that hungry, after finding what they wanted they spotted a couple of 14 ounces of orange juice,

By ten o'clock that morning they had caught the bus to the shopping center again, then after about four hours of doing nothing but shopping they caught the same bus back again with their arms loaded down with all sorts of parcels to take back to Canada. That day was mostly spent laying around in the their bathing suits sun tanning on the patio, until it got too hot to be in the sun any longer. Blossom cuddled up to Wesley on his single bed and they had another sleep that afternoon, when there finally awake and refreshed again they were back dressed by seven P.M. Wesley flipped a coin to see where they would eat dinner, by that time the both of them were getting hungry, Wesley won, they went out to Mr. Mikes Broil Your Own Steaks, that was an unusual way to eat out, but enjoyable evening with steaks and salads from the salad bar.

Then the reporter asked Blossom as she was rocking back and fourth remembering the good old days on her front porch, "What did you both do after that"? As Blossom was remembering the candle lit restaurant at Mr. Mikes she spoke softly, we just walked through some more dress shops, Wesley use to like buying her pretty gowns and things.

Blossom continued to say, "By the time Wesley, my sweet husband was getting pretty tired bless his soul," So Blossom would say," they just walked back through the market place and were back in their hotel room by ten-thirty that evening.

Being the next day a Saturday they were up a eleven then dressed for the day in the appropriate clothing, Blossom dressed into her sleek sleeveless sun dress with a floppy hat to match, this also matched Wesley's Hawaiian short sleeved shirt, Blossom liked to match Wesley, it didn't matter to him as long as he had something to wear, this is for what I understood from her the reporter would say.

After Blossom had said, "They had breakfast up in their little room again and then out to the aquarium and back to the market place, which Wesley and Blossom enjoyed tremendously seeing the different exhibits.

Blossom had told the reporter that she had found this beautiful short sleeved dark green printed sun dress for herself and to match the short sleeved green shirt Wesley had just finished purchasing a second before hand, then they browsed a little more and came across matching sun dress and short sleeve shirts to match for Bonny and Darcy back home. Wesley and Blossom looked at each other then smiled and nodded their head in approval to buy them and would bring them back on the plane to surprise the children with them.

That afternoon when they finally arrived back at their hotel room around three-thirty, then both had a bath to cool down and Wesley offered to wash Blossom's back for her, he was always so gently when washing her back. Blossom liked having her back washed with his strong but gently hands.

When the two of them were finally freshened up from the hot stickiness of the day, they had supper out at Tom's place, it was located on the ground floor of their hotel, on one end was the eating area and the other end of the room was the bar with a TV located above the bar on the wall just like you would see in the movies. That evening was spent relaxing in front of a black and white TV which was brought up earlier by one of the bell hops.

The next day all sun shinny out, they got up early again, caught the bus to the Al a Moana shopping center. Blossom always managed to get her way with Wesley she go on to say, I guess she said that he was butter in her hands. That sunny day was especially well enjoyed the two of them did all sorts of little things, like they saw a little kids hula show, Wesley really liked that one, He always did love little children though, Blossom would say, remembering the expression on his face while watching the little ones doing their hula show, this was taking place in the middle of the mall in amongst the crowd of people by the escalators, Blossom believed that Wesley was visualizing his own children up there on stage, When the hula show was all over Wesley found a small but quaint little restaurant just outside the shopping area in which they both were ready to sit down from and rest their weary feet, it was a nice quiet lunch they had.

After lunch they did some more shopping for the family back home, then to the hotel room loaded down with more parcels, it was a long bus ride back to the Sand Castle Hotel, That same evening they had supper at the Out rigger at about five P.M. then came back, this time they took the long way back just in order to be able to strolled along the beach in the moon lit for awhile, late that evening they sent out for pizza, watched some TV while making sweet passionate love on one of the single beds. That room had twin beds instead of one double to sleep in.

The following morning Blossom woke up with a cold, they had breakfast then back along the beach side, the two of them walked for miles for a long time, Blossom loved to walk along the beach in her bare feet with Wesley at her side. At that point was when Wesley spoke up and said, "it was getting harder and harder to find something to do in the days to come, their funds were almost all gone and they had four more days to go After giving it a great deal of thought they had decided to catch the number eight bus to Ala Moana shopping center again, after shopping for what seemed to be a mighty long time and ending up without buying anything, they then decided to have lunch at the same quaint little restaurant, then caught the bus back to the hotel room where they took it easy for awhile from the scorching sun.

Around about five-thirty Wesley went out and brought back some Chinese food for dinner, which they ate on their hotel balcony, up there on the balcony, they had a beautiful view of the lagoon. When Wesley and Blossom finally finished their meals, it was getting pretty boring just sitting around, so they caught the Ala Moana bus; back to the shopping center where there they watched the annual Chinese Queen contest. The contestants came down the escalator about three steps apart from each other, very graceful and very proud, held their heads up high, the girls were all around the age of nineteen to twenty-one, they were wearing bright red shinny satin type gowns that fit fairly snug to their bodies, but before they would pick the queen they had to lite those fire crackers, there must of been around a couple of hundred all in that huge wooden crate that had been covered with a mesh type wire top. It was just like the fourth of July, very pretty, exclaimed Blossom. When the contest was finally finished, they caught the bus back to the hotel room and went right off to sleep.

The very next morning started off pretty well like the other mornings, they walked down to the Ala Moana shopping center again, but when they finally arrived back to the hotel, Wesley discovered that the couple who had occupied the room across from them, who also had won the trip from another contest, had to leave real sudden to go back to Canada, since they had just received a long distance phone call from a friend who was taking care of their six month old baby boy, had phoned to say that their son had passed away the night before in his sleep from crib death. That couple still had their return tickets, but the stay time in Hawaii wasn't up for another three days and the airport personal in charge that day wouldn't honor their tickets three days early, even though it was an emergency. That poor young couple had to come back up to the hotel and figure out how to raise enough money to go home early on that day. In the evening they finally called a friend in Canada and asked them to please wire them enough money down to them to get their return tickets for the next available flight home, unfortunately they wouldn't receive the money until the next morning, so they left bright in early the following day very sad.

January Twentieth, Blossom and Wesley had gotten up to go and get dressed around eleven in the morning after making beautiful love in their hotel room for over an hour. They then caught the bus to Pearl Harbor docks, where they had lunch while waiting for the shuttle boat to take them over to the memorial ship, the Arizona that had gone down with so many men aboard. While waiting on the Be docks, they met a very nice couple (negro) named Alice and Albert, Alice and Albert caught the same shuttle boat to go over to the memorial. In the course of talking they exchanged addresses. Blossom gave them a picture of Wesley and herself, which in return they did the same for Blossom. At seven-o-five Wesley and Blossom were back watching Adam Twelve on the black and white TV in their own hotel room, being it too hot again outside. That was how they had spent the afternoon, just watching TV and making sweet passionate love all day. The next day a Thursday they had gotten up and dressed by ten-thirty, had breakfast then caught the bus back to the Ala Moana shopping center once more. First they stopped at the photographers to pick up Blossom's film, then they walked for awhile and then Wesley bought Blossom a beautiful orchard to wear as a corsage. She came across some real nice smelling perfume called ginger, so she had decided to purchase it for Wesley's sister back home.

The next morning around one A.M. they were both woken up, or should I say the whole hotel was woken up by a bus load of young teenagers playing their guitars and just hooting and howling at the top of their lunges.

Blossom and Wesley were awaken again around eleven in the morning and at that, they decided to stay up and go window shopping, when they had gotten back to the hotel room that morning, Blossom decided to get some of their dirty clothes washed at the closest laundry-mat, which was just around the corner of them.

Come evening Wesley decided to take Blossom for a walk through the zoo and then to the down town of Hawaii. On the way back from their stroll Blossom had pressed Wesley to go through the market place one more time, there she bought a Ti-plant to take back to Canada, the plant was only ninety-nine cents.

The same evening when they returned back to the hotel room Blossom had gotten everything ready for their trip back to Canada the very next morning.

Next morning, they were ready at the front entrance of the hotel for their shuttle ride in a long black coach type vehicle to take them back to the airport, once at the airport their luggage was tagged and then sent on its way.

Before they were to enter the plane once again they waited in turn to walk through a metal detector that could tell if you had any weapons. It was thirty-two below outside the plane and five hours flying time back to Canada, the part of Canada that Wesley and Blossom were going back to, the weather report read cloudy. By eight o'clock it was forty degrees and eight miles an hour winds.

As Wesley and Blossom were heading into the Canadian airport it was fifty-two degrees outside the plane at nine-thirty in the evening. The plane was traveling at a speed of five hundred-eighty miles per hour that had dropped from thirty-five thousand feet to thirty-five hundred feet. All the stewardesses were on strike at the time of coming home, so the stewards wives helped out in serving the passengers, making them feel comfortable on their flight home. The meal was very delicious; Blossom had red wine with her meal. The plane arrived at the Canadian airport around twelve-ten in the early morning, Wesley's brother and his wife came to pick them up, then Blossom gave out the gifts that were picked so carefully out for each one from Hawaii, after that they just went straight to bed and slept for a long while before picking up the children.

Was up by ten-thirty Canada's time, phoned the Cartwright's and talked to Bonny and Darcy, Wesley played his Arizona record on the hi-fi, after lunch they went back to the airport to make arrangements to have Blossom's luggage repaired, since in Hawaii they wouldn't have it fixed. Around seven-thirty in the evening they went out to see Blossom's parents, Sheila and her family were also there waiting to give Wesley and Blossom a big welcome home greeting, then Blossom sat in the middle of the living room floor with all her relatives around her as she and Wesley presented them with their gifts from Hawaii that had been specially picked out for each one with great pleasure.

The following day being a Tuesday they were both awake and up at ten-thirty, Wesley took Bonny with him while Darcy stayed home with Blossom and they house cleaned, or should I say Blossom house cleaned as fast as Darcy messed it up.

Blossom got back onto the phone to her clients, she had arranged to phone on her day back from their trip, she then arranged up about four Tupperware parties for the following week, then made lunch for Darcy and herself, played the record she had bought in the night club. After Darcy had a little nap, Blossom phoned the repair shop office and found that she could pick up her Tupperware suit case tomorrow around ten in the morning.

The following day was a busy day for them, after breakfast they picked up the suitcase, took the sunbeam mix master back to the store, the store was very kind about giving her money for it, since she had won it in a Tupperware contest and didn't need one, being she all ready owned a real good one. With the money Blossom had received from the mix master, she had bought groceries for the family, it was only twenty-three dollars, but it was better than no groceries at all.

By six-thirty Blossom took her car and left for her seven-thirty Tupperware party, she had arranged a couple of days before hand. Blossom had to travel all the way out to Harvey road, stayed around two hours demonstrating Tupperware and sold around fifty-eight dollars, then packed up and left to go home, after recording her Tupperware sales for the evening she then sat and cuddled up next to Wesley and watched some TV, he had waited up for her, then they both went to bed tired.

Wesley started out early for the job the next morning, while Blossom stayed home with Bonny and Darcy, she then got up her fifth party over the phone. Blossom was very proud of herself, because her Tupperware team would now make their goal in Tupperware sales and parties. After what she had figured was enough telephoning customers, Blossom washed the kitchen floor and did some laundry. By one-thirty Tiki their cock-a-Poo female dog was all ready having her puppies, so far the first one was born dead, she was having lots of trouble having them this time. Blossom had kept a close watch on her in case she needed any help. That evening when Wesley arrived home, supper was on the table and Tiki had six pups, four males and two females that lived.

Chapter Twelve

The Home Coming

    Friday, after they had been back from their Hawaiian trip for awhile, it turned out to be the biggest day that the radio station had changed over at two-o-six that evening to more wattage. Wesley took Bonny to work that morning with him. Blossom got another Tupperware party up, then the hippies who bought the old chicken coop of a house out back of the alley had just backed all the way up Blossom's back lawn, after the yard had just been freshly rained on the night before, their blue and white with a V-line mark on the right side of their truck and camper had made a huge hole half way up the back lawn.
    At the time it happened Blossom was too scared to say anything, since they were big grizzly looking guys, who were a lot bigger and meaner than she was." Blossom was more worried about her mother then, Dawn had been getting quite a few dizzy spells lately and they didn't know what was causing them.
    After supper, Wesley picked a fight with Blossom, one of their biggest fights since they were married, Wesley ended up sleeping on the couch. Blossom had moved the heavy old cherry wood dresser in front of the bedroom door, so Wesley couldn't open up the bedroom door since they didn't have a lock on it. Wesley couldn't get in so he had to sleep on the couch, Blossom threw out his pajamas and pillow and blanket before she moved the dresser in front of the door. Blossom had said she had done that so Wesley had to learn a lesson, that he can't always have his way all the time. Blossom had thought about them fighting all night long, the very next morning she got up early, so not to miss Wesley and to be able to apologize to him. Blossom usually did do the apologizing just to keep peace in the family, she said she was that way growing up too, if there was a fight down stairs and she was up stairs, she would stay up there until the fight was all over with.

Blossom didn't like to see her husband go off to work in a bitter mood, she felt that maybe someday when she would say good-bye to him in the morning when he went off to work, at one point that he might end up in a car accident and never be able to return back home again, so she always liked to give Wesley a kiss good-bye in the morning to patch things up from the night before so he would be in a better frame of mind while out working.

She said she always wanted to remember him in a happy mood, the same with Wesley; he was to be able to remember Blossom in a happy mood too, if anything should happen to either one of them while away from each other that day.

Next day being a Saturday, Wesley drove Blossom all over the city to pick up Tupperware for replacements, then to the bank and back to the store to exchange Darcy's sleepwear. That evening they had a terrific night making love, making up from the fight the night before, they were making passionate love all night long, finally they fell off to sleep around two in the morning, only to wake up to the sound of kids playing outside under their bedroom window.

Wesley spent that day helping Blossom wash floors and taking the baby buggy back to Sheila's. When they had arrived at Sheila's place, she invited them in to stay for supper, but they had a previous invitation to have supper at the Bailey's home that evening. In that Wesley just took a rain check for his family on the dinner invitation. After the dinner was well over with and the dishes done, Wesley's dad gave him a hair cut on the stool in the old farm like kitchen, the stool was placed near the kitchen table and back door, Mr. Bailey had to be very careful when cutting Wesley's hair, since he had a large brown mole on the right side of his head, just hidden under his hair line above his ear.

What a hectic day Monday turned out to be, it started off when Blossom didn't get too much sleep the night before, she had to leave the house at about eight-thirty in the morning, then forgot her Tupperware badge at home, which all the Tupperware dealers had to wear at the meetings, Blossom had to come all the way back home after which she had all ready driven half way across town to the meeting hall.

Then had to pick up some Tupperware on her way down to be replaced, the meeting started at nine-thirty in the morning, she ended up being fifteen minutes late, then after the meeting she left for the office, the office and the meeting place were about one mile down the road to pick up her Tupperware from the warehouse. Blossom then had to wait thirty minutes in line for those orders, around eleven-thirty or a quarter to twelve she finally finished picking up her orders and loading them into her small Toyota station wagon. Blossom was getting pretty hungry by then, but she had another meeting to go to yet. That meeting was called Stop-N-Go, it was a program for the Tupperware dealers who had wished to up grade themselves to a manager position, and the program was all free to them.

The Stop-N-Go meeting finished around two-fifteen in the late afternoon, then she delivered some Tupperware replacements on her way home, Blossom got home around three-o'clock in the late afternoon just in time to unload all the Tupperware boxes from her car and go to pick up the children from the baby sitters, at that time it was her sister-n-law who was kind enough to do the baby sitting with the children for her. Jan also had two children of her own at the time and they were about six month's difference in age than Blossom's children. Wesley made supper that evening while Blossom was busy packing her Tupperware orders in the middle of the tiny living room floor, they had to be packed individually into each order and then into each party group." She mentioned," the rest of the evening she had some of those awful migraine headaches she usually got on a Monday. On the following day being a Tuesday, Blossom spent a lot of the time on the phone trying to get some parties up for the week to follow, she always felt energetic on the following day from the meeting. By noon she had no luck with her Tupperware parties, Blossom just then decided to give the phoning a rest for awhile and do some laundry, that she had been putting off for some time now. Blossom had started the laundry when Bonny woke up from her afternoon nap, then they got two more loads done up before Darcy had woken up from his nap. Blossom then got the children ready to play in the fenced back yard and then sat down at her sewing machine and started to sew on the double quilt she was making for some time now from scrapes of material and clothing that had been worn out, she had started making that quilt when she was expecting Bonny and now Bonny was one year old. Wesley was late coming home that evening he had been held up in traffic, there was a car accident that had happened on the bridge around rush hour four-thirty and the traffic was only able to crawl. At that point Wesley mentioned that the cupboards were starting to look rather bare and their money was running out fast, He only had maybe four days more of work left to go on that job sight. Unless Blossom could get up some more Tupperware parties they weren't going to have any money in the house at all. "Tupperware dealers have an old saying amongst themselves," It was the husbands who brought in the bread and butter, the wives only brought in the dessert," which meant that in Tupperware you don't make enough money to live on to support your family, but every penny counts. Blossom got on the phone the following morning to try to generate some income into their household funds, lucky Bonny went to bed that afternoon without any trouble, she usually was the one that would keep Darcy awake and fool around when they were supposed to be sleeping, one afternoon when they were supposed to be sleeping, Darcy and Bonny took off their mattress from the youth bed and braced it against the door to make a barricade, they were only maybe three and four years old at the time. Wesley and Blossom both had to pry open the door that time. Blossom managed to get two parties booked up, but they were both for in the future, one in the middle of the next month and the other one even further on down the line. Wesley was home by four-thirty that evening; he had got paid his last cheque, so he took them out to buy a few groceries that evening. After the grocery shopping was all finished they went straight home, unloaded the groceries and put them all away, then Blossom made supper and they just relaxed in front of the TV.

The rest of the week went much the same way, Blossom got up, seen Wesley off in the morning to go and look for work, then she had fed the children breakfast, made the beds, did up the laundry and cleaned the rest of the house up, including cleaning out the bird cage, then by the time Wesley had arrived home for supper it was all ready on the table for him.

Come Sunday they got up in time to go to church, after the church services they were back home in time for Blossom to make lunch, she had made soup and sandwiches that time, Wesley helped her after lunch with the dishes and then put the children down for a little nap, Blossom laid down with Darcy for awhile. Woke up in time to make supper again and then watch TV for awhile and went straight to bed early. Monday was the same old routine in the morning, taking the children to the baby sitters, then off to the Tupperware meeting by nine-thirty. On the way to the meeting Blossom had to pick up another lady, that had made arrangements with her earlier in the week to take part in that particular meeting, there was a lot of special surprise for everyone that morning handed out.

After the meeting was finished, Blossom dropped off her lady friend at her home and then picked up the children and went into town to pick up some dog food while in town she paid a utility bill.

Wesley had gone to the doctors earlier and then onto the unemployment office after which he went straight to the union building to see about a job on the board. That same evening the Cartwright's dropped in, they all had a very pleasant evening chatting, Casey offered Wesley a job working for him again building houses.

On the next morning Wesley was up and ready to go to work for Casey. Blossom stayed home with the children that day and cleaned up the house, by seven-thirty that evening, Wesley was home and they all sat down to a very nice meal, around eight o'clock in the evening some friends dropped in and we played a game called easy money, that game was something like monopoly, we played it until eleven o'clock, then said their good-byes to their friends and went to bed themselves. Wesley was back into hard labor and his back was feeling much better then. They were up early again the next morning and Blossom got one Tupperware party up for the end of the month. She also wrote to their friends in California, the ones they met while in Hawaii. A nice size cheque also arrived in the mail for Wesley that afternoon, then Blossom came down with very bad cold and didn't know how she was going to make the Tupperware parties that were all ready arranged for the following evening. On the next day, one of those days where you should have stayed in bed all day, Blossom woke up with her cold being worse than the day before and the children then decided to get into all kinds of trouble, by the time that Wesley came home she had all ready eaten and was ready to go out the front door for her Tupperware party. The party was a success, Blossom came home around ten that evening and Wesley was still waiting up for her, She had sold over one-hundred dollars and forty cents worth of Tupperware, there were two kind ladies who booked a party which with in the thirty day requirements time for the hostess to receive her gift free.

Blossom was in bed by eleven-thirty, but couldn't sleep she was still awake at eight in the morning and by nine-thirty she had to get up, Boy! Was she ever tired that day? Friday almost the end of the month was Blossom ever glad, she was so surprised, the children actually were being good that afternoon. Sheila wasn't working too far from their home then, so she came over for lunch, then the furnace went off. Blossom phoned Wesley, he told her what to do and she got the furnace working again. In the mean time the children were fast asleep, bless their little hearts, Blossom managed to do some Tupperware phoning after Sheila left to go back to work at the bank, but she had no luck in getting any parties up for the future. Wesley never got home until eight o'clock that evening. A fellow worker gave him a TV set free to take home and do what ever he could do with it, so if it was free Wesley brought it home, he hoped to fix it and sell it to help pay some bills.

Saturday they were up around nine-thirty left the house with Bonny and Darcy around eleven A.M. decided then to deliver some Tupperware and purchase a dog license, off to the Bailey's house and then onto the department store way down town to purchase a pair of boots for Darcy.

Coming home they ended up with a flat tire in the middle of the down town sector. When Wesley had finally replaced the tire with the spare in the trunk, they went to another department store where there Wesley bought every one lunch, after lunch went straight home to watch some TV. Sunday morning after church they came home and changed into their working clothes, Wesley and Blossom washed and waxed all the floors in the house, then they both cleaned the car inside and out until it just shone. Blossom made a rolled brisket and potatoes with green vegetables for dinner, for dessert she brought out one of her apple pies from the freezer, Blossom usually baked in quantities and then froze them for later. After supper they took the time left that evening easy, Wesley helped Blossom with the supper dishes, and then put the children down to sleep, after which they just cuddled up on the old couch together watching their favorite program. The following Monday morning Blossom left the house at eight-thirty to pick up the ladies, after delivering Bonny and Darcy to the baby sitters again. One of the two ladies didn't show up to the place arranged to meet, Blossom just went without her and took June, they arrived at the meeting a little after the meeting had all ready started, around quarter to ten, found a seat near the back of the room with her unit and then there was the spell down, that was a little game the dealers and managers played every Monday morning at the meetings, the highest dealer of the week in sales use to win a gift from the distributor manager. Blossom was the highest for the week with over eight hundred dollars in sales; she had won herself a casserole dish, beverage jug and a set of six Tupperware tumblers in harvest gold color. After the meeting Blossom took June home and then out to the bank, after which she picked up the children again. When Wesley arrived home just in time for supper, Blossom had all that good news to tell him. After supper the Cartwright's phoned them to invite them over to play a game of pool at their home, that was the men played a game of pool, Sheila and Grant were there too, Casey had purchased a brand new car and wanted everyone to see it. When everyone was finished having a ride in the new car, they went inside and chatted for awhile, then the children were getting cranky and tired so Wesley took his little family home and Blossom put the children to bed. Wesley didn't have to go to work the next day, Blossom had asked him if he would take the children to the zoo, which he did, in the mean time it was so peaceful in the house without the children always under foot.

Blossom decided to get back onto the phone and try to get some more Tupperware parties up for the following week, She managed to get three outside dustings, that was what it was called when booking a Tupperware party over the phone instead of through a Tupperware party, she still hadn't been able to shake that cold of hers, Now Wesley was home with the Bonny and Darcy and Darcy had come down with the same cold and runs that afternoon. By one-thirty the mailman came around with some disturbing news, the hydro company was shutting off the power tomorrow; apparently they had said that Wesley hadn't paid his hydro bill, when in fact he had paid it a week before hand. Wesley was pretty upset over that letter with two people in the house down with colds and now they want to shut off his hydro. There was nothing he could do just then, so by eleven-thirty they went to bed, the next morning first thing he went straight down to the hydro office to try and straighten out the mistake made by their company.

When he had arrived back home that afternoon just in time for lunch, he told Blossom that everything was going to be all right. Apparently they had some mix up with their computer and the girl behind the desk promised to straighten it all out for him. After lunch the children went out in the back yard to play, Wesley got busy painting the master bedroom green, but it was too dark of a green so he had to mix it with white paint in order to tone it down a bit.

Blossom wasn't much of a painter, so she just stayed clear out of his way and went on the phone trying to get some more Tupperware parties up, she managed to get three more, then in the evening she had a Tupperware party out in the country, Wesley drove her, since when it was so far out, Blossom didn't like to drive in the evening after dark by herself. She was always afraid of getting lost. That party wasn't very good having to travel so far out. The party was only ninety-six dollars and that included tax. On the following morning she was up by ten-thirty, Wesley had finished painting the bedroom. She managed to do some Tupperware phoning after Sheila left to go home. Blossom phoned on Tupperware parties, then mailed some letters, drove down to the department store, did a little shopping with the children, three in the afternoon, she was home again. By five o'clock Bonny and Blossom had gone to a fast food restaurant to pick up some supper. Wesley went to bed at seven that evening, he said, "I'm not feeling too well Blossom I think I will turn in early." Blossom figured that he was maybe coming down with the same cold she been having for the last week.

Darcy still had the runs and his cold wasn't getting any better Blossom mentioned earlier, "she been just plain pooped out." On the following day she really didn't know what to do anymore, "yesterday Wesley wasn't feeling too well, she took good care of him and he spent most of the day in bed sleeping, today Blossom wasn't feeling too well, but did he care, "No he invites his parents over for a visit.

Well Blossom did the laundry, the house cleaning and made all the meals, but sure wished that her cold would have gone away by then, by eleven-thirty when all the company had left she went straight to bed.

On the next afternoon Wesley worked for his sister and brother-n-law at their home, while Blossom delivered some replacements, and picked up Tupperware, Wesley had taken Bonny with him, while Blossom had Darcy that afternoon. Around four in the late afternoon she had to pick up Wesley and Bonny since she had their only car for the day, came home and made supper together.

The children went to bed at seven that evening, then the two of them just sat around in the living room relaxing in front of a crackling fire, morning Bonny went with her daddy back to his brother-n-laws to finish up the work, they had lunch over there and around four-thirty he drove in the yard with two plants for Blossom, one was a tulip and the other one was a hyacinth plant. The following morning Blossom slept until ten-thirty, got up fed the children and went back to bed until one o'clock in the afternoon, she had said, that she just didn't have any energy at all that day

In the evening when Wesley came home he saw how bad Blossom was feeling and he made the meal and fed the children their supper, then he even did up the supper dishes for her, while Blossom just tried to see if she could sleep that darn cold off, she had no appetite at all that day. Later on that evening Blossom couldn't get back to sleep, so she got up and beat Wesley in a game of checkers, by seven o'clock she had almost for gotten to pick another lady up to go to her mother-n-laws for a unit meeting, Mrs. Bailey was Blossom's manager in Tupperware at the time, by eight o'clock that same evening was the time set for the unit meeting. Blossom figured that she might have a chance of being unit princess and receiving the unit princess pin, that would mean a lot to Blossom. The pin was shaped like a crown in light blue and white with rhinestones surrounding the name. She was very tired when she finally arrived home at eleven-thirty that evening. On the following morning Bonny turned up sick like the rest of the family had been. So they didn't go to church that morning. Blossom was still trying to get over her cold; they just took it easy that sunny Sunday at home.

On Monday morning Blossom was feeling up to going to the Tupperware meeting across the bridge, they had showed the jubilee slides that morning and one of the managers was leaving for Hawaii to go in three weeks time. Then Blossom went to the warehouse and picked up one hundred eighty-eight dollars worth of Tupperware, Blossom was home around two in the afternoon that day. Wesley had the children so she didn't have to worry about picking up the children on time from the baby sitters. After she was home for about an hour, Wesley took Bonny and they went to the unemployment office for work.

In the mean time Blossom had Darcy sleeping while she was packing her Tupperware orders in the middle of the small living room again. When the Tupperware was all packed and out of the way, Darcy woke up, Blossom then got him all dressed so by the time that Wesley had arrived home that afternoon they all went into town after a quick bite to eat.

Wesley had showed Blossom the stained glass he wanted to put in the china cabinet, he had just finished making for their anniversary awhile back, that piece of stained glass was for the top hutch in the sliding doors. It was harvest gold in color with a pebbly surface. After seeing the glass and how expensive it was they went home, Blossom made supper, by the time they had sat down to eat it was getting pretty late.

On Tuesday Blossom did some more phoning, but she had no luck in raising any Tupperware parties up. She figured that maybe it was because of the time of the year being around the end of February.

Bonny was still complaining of stomachaches, then she went with her daddy to his sister's home and apparently Bonny had disappeared from Wesley in town, she was only around three years old at the time, the police had found her pushing a shopping cart in the local grocery store, after Wesley had looked everywhere for her, even at the post office where her grandfather Bailey worked, Bonny was loading up all kinds of fruits in her grocery cart. The police knew her grandfather Bailey in the post office which wasn't too far from the grocery store she was in, so they just brought her over to him and there was where Wesley had found her, then he brought her straight home, Bonny thought she was being a big girl and doing the grocery shopping like mummy does. Wesley was furious with her. By seven-thirty Blossom was to be at a customer's home for a Tupperware party that evening. After playing a few games she then sold over one hundred dollars and had two more parties booked for the future, by that time it was time to leave for home again, so She packed all the Tupperware and orders forms back into the two suit cases; the company provided for her and drove home. She had arrived home just in time to discover that Bonny and Darcy had wrecked her only tea kettle; they had filled it up with powdered milk and then plugged it in. Wesley was all the more furious with his children then, that night, He was trying to fix the wrecked tea kettle, they ended up going to bed rather late and not getting it fixed. Wednesday came around and was spent delivering Tupperware to the different customers and collecting the money from them. Around lunch time Blossom treated the family out to a Roy Rogers restaurant, then they priced a new tea kettle, since it was impossible for them to fix the old one, By four in the afternoon they were headed back with their brand new tea kettle, had supper then went out to a another Tupperware party again, that time she ended up selling only thirty-six dollars with only three people attending the party, as Blossom would say "Not bad Hey!" She arrived home around eleven-thirty as Blossom always tried to keep her parties short. She watched TV with Wesley, who was still waiting up for her. Bonny went with Wesley the next morning while Darcy stayed home with is mummy. Blossom washed all the floors in the house and then Darcy tried to help dust. Just after lunch she put Darcy down for his afternoon nap then she washed and set her hair. After an hour or so Darcy woke up and Blossom gave him his bath, then Wesley and Bonny came home, the mailman showed up just after Wesley had arrived home, he had brought the pictures that were taken in Hawaii, when they were all finished looking through them with the children, they all went out grocery shopping, she spent sixty dollars and eighty cents for two weeks. That same afternoon Blossom got a lot of calls as, she had put an ad in the local paper on help wanted in recruiting new Tupperware dealers, you see they had a contest going on and the one who recruited the most dealers got a terrific gift.

 She had another Tupperware party that same evening, that time it was just a small one, not too far from their home, Blossom had sold only forty-eight dollars, and no future bookings, Blossom was home by eleven that evening and went straight to bed. The next morning was when Blossom had decided to hold a open house Tupperware party in her own home, she had sent the children with Wesley about twelve-thirty, then Sheila came over at one o'clock that afternoon, when she had finally left, Blossom started setting up the card table that Wesley's parents had given them awhile back. Blossom set the card table up in front of the fire place in the living room where there would be plenty of light on the display of Tupperware. The order forms had been placed around on each chair, then she set up the paper cups and paper plates with chips and cookies, finally a beverage to help themselves at. Blossom had started the open house around one-thirty and it was to end around three in the afternoon when Wesley was to come home, but no one showed up for the open house at all. Blossom was very up set about the whole ordeal, so then she got a brain wave, she started phoning her different customers to see if they needed anything from the Tupperware catalog. Blossom got some orders, not many, but enough to call it a Tupperware party. Wesley and the children arrived home in time for supper, they had brought chicken and buns home for supper, all in all Blossom said, "It was a very trying day."

The following day was Willett's birthday, she was seventeen now, Blossom delivered some Tupperware then went to the bank to deposit money and pick up some more Tupperware replacements in town. She was home by three in the afternoon, then on the phone again and brought herself in more orders for the open house Tupperware party, which brought her party up to one hundred dollars and forty cents including two other bookings for the future. In the whole week she had sold two hundred twenty-nine dollars and forty-eight cents. Wesley took the family out to a fast food restaurant for supper, he was still out of work, but he figured that Blossom had been working too hard and that would give her a break. Blossom said, "she sure wished that her husband would hurry up and get a job," On the following evening being a Sunday, Dawn had asked everyone to come and help celebrate Willett's birthday a day late. Blossom had baked Willette a birthday cake and decorated it with all the trimmings, after the meal was finished and the dishes were out of the way, Willette started opening up her presents. Blossom still hadn't got a hold of one of her Tupperware hostess for the next evening, but she had two possible recruits coming to the meeting with her on Monday morning. The children were on their best behavior that evening. Dawn had told Blossom to go look after her kids, while they all went down stairs to play pool. Blossom had wished she could learn how to play pool, so she brought Bonny and Darcy down with her, since everyone else had a chance to play pool too.

By midnight they had arrived home, went to sleep and early the next morning she was up ready for the Tupperware meeting. At the meeting Blossom had thought for sure she had two recruits, they were so excited about joining the Tupperware team, the only problem was the girls were only fifteen and sixteen years old, the age limit was eighteen to become a dealer. Blossom also was able to win a set of two dish cloths with her draw ticket; she needed them very much at the time. After the Tupperware meeting was all over, Blossom had stopped in for the Tupperware prospective manager meeting at the office, and then she took the girls home and arrived home her self around one in the afternoon very tired. She had been thinking quite strongly about becoming a Tupperware manager. Her mother-n-law was one and now she was thinking about doing it too. The mangers have to have at least six recruits working under them before they can become a manager, this was why Blossom was trying so hard to get up more recruits in the last week or so, she all ready had three. When the dealers do become managers they receive a bouquet of red roses and a brand new Ford station wagon in their choice of color, all power and everything for convenience included. Blossom knew now that if she still had that petit-mal she would never have been able to get this far in life and she thanks God everyday for being healthy again. Wesley had discussed this matter with her before and he had told Blossom he didn't mind if that was what she really wanted to do. It meant a lot more work for her, but also more money would come into this house for paying bills. You see when you become a manager you earn what you sell plus a percentage from the working girls. After Blossom sorted out the Tupperware she had just brought home, she then made dinner and brought in the laundry from outside on the close line, then hangs another load up, and after that it was bed time.

In the morning she did some more phone calling for Tupperware parties, only after Blossom had the children all dressed and fed, the dishes out of the way and her house cleaned from top to bottom. Wesley went job hunting again, then Darcy decided to take off and he walked down to the end of the not so busy street, in which the mailman had brought him back home on his way delivering the mail. By three in the afternoon Wesley was home and they all went out to the department store, Blossom didn't find what she had been looking for, so they went home again. That same evening Wesley and Blossom never got to bed until one-thirty in the morning, they were so busy packing Tupperware together into individual orders for each party, Blossom had four large parties to pack and they all had to be delivered by the next day. Blossom woke up around seven in the morning, then looked in on the children and said what! The Heck, and crawled back into bed with Wesley. After that they didn't wake up until eleven that morning, when Wesley got up and was ready to go to his sister's place again. The next time she saw Wesley was when he came home for lunch and Blossom was in the middle of washing the kitchen floor, after lunch he took Bonny with him to his sister's. Blossom put Darcy down to sleep and about after an hour he woke up, they both walked down to mail a letter at the end of the second street close by.

The following morning they were all up by nine-thirty, had breakfast, then Wesley went to his brother's to get his car fixed, his brother was a great person for fixing the cars. Bonny and Darcy stayed home and played outside all afternoon, while Blossom was back on the phone generating clients again. She had managed to get one Tupperware party booked, just in time for Wesley to arrive home, and then Bonny and Blossom took the car and went delivering Tupperware, while Wesley stayed home with Darcy. By the time she had gotten home that afternoon, Wesley had all ready had supper cooked and placed on the table for her. After supper they all sat around in the living room and looked at some Hawaiian pictures, then at seven-thirty the children were put down to sleep for the night. Wesley just watched a little TV with Blossom, which ended up retiring earlier than usual, and ending up making beautiful love then an hour later starting up all over again until the wee hours in the morning Blossom didn't do too much the following day, but she did how ever manager to get one dating that had phoned her up that afternoon for a Tupperware party, after that she and Wesley played a game of poker until Bonny and Darcy had woken up, so they all sat around the fire place in the living room watching TV and eating popcorn. On the next day the time they finally arrived home late that afternoon, Blossom and the children laid down for a bit of a sleep, then Blossom got up only after she had heard Wesley screaming outside under their bedroom window at her to come and help him with the car, that was around seven in the evening. Later his dad came over and helped him reverse the brake shoes on the car. The children were up by then and they both came out to see their grandfather, then around nine they were both put back down again to sleep. The rest of the week went much the same, except Blossom did mange to sell two more pups for five dollars each, she still had four pups left to sell. On the following Sunday morning she made everyone their favorite pancake with syrup, then by supper time Wesley had brought a sixteen inch pizza home for dinner. Tuesday what tiring day, it started when Blossom no sooner brought all the laundry in off the line outside from out back, when it began to rain and it rained like cats and dogs. After lunch she put Darcy down to sleep in his crib and Bonny down in her youth bed, Bonny felt like such a big girl since she got her youth bed, then by three in the afternoon Wesley came home Blossom was on the phone all afternoon while the children were fast asleep. In the evening they all went out, Blossom got herself a free facial, only she ended up buying the darn make-up for eighteen dollars. The following day was the same routine, she washed the kitchen floor and walls, then did the laundry, Wesley's brother Rod and his wife Jan came over around two-thirty, then by five the Cartwright's had arrived for dinner. After dinner was all through and Dawn had helped Blossom clear away the dishes, they all sat around the kitchen table and played a good old fashion game of crib. Blossom was saying, "you don't see too much of that game crib played with this younger generation now days." By then Wesley had found himself a job working in construction again, then the following Monday wasn't the best of days for him, to start with Wesley's boss didn't phone the inspector until nine A.M. by ten after nine Wesley had taken the children down to Jan's while Blossom was at her Tupperware meeting across town. After that he decided to go to his boss's home, by noon Wesley had discovered that he had lost his lunch, so he ended up working all day without any lunch to tide him over until supper time.

    Blossom had been late for the meeting that morning, when it was finished she had to hurry home to unload the Tupperware boxes in order for there to be any room in the small station wagon for the children, which she had to go to pick up soon. After picking up the children she had to deliver some more Tupperware and then she decided to take a break and go over to see her parent's new home. The very next day was another one of those rush-around days, between the kids getting into trouble and Blossom trying to keep her neighbor as a recruit, then trying to get more Tupperware parties up, it was just too much for her.

Wesley never got home until seven that evening and they ended up with cranky children and a late cold dinner. By the end of March they managed to sell two more pups which helped out in paying the bills, Blossom made a Irish stew and a jello for dinner, then she sat down at the kitchen table and wrote her aunt a letter, Blossom hadn't written to her for about two months. After about a week of steady phoning she finally got some afternoon outside dating up. Blossom had found a moment in the late afternoon for her to have an hour or so rest, since she hadn't been feeling well those days, She had stomach cramps and very bad back aches, they were caused by her menstruation periods which she had started early that morning. Wesley arrived home early that afternoon, but he had to put in a half day on Saturday with two other co-workers. As they chatted at the dinner table about his job, Blossom mentioned that they were invited over to her parents that evening, as tired as Wesley was they all went after dinner. Willette was still living at home then, but she did have a steady boy friend. Saturday Wesley went to work as planned and boy! Was he upset, no one turned up except one other fellow, so they decided to work for an hour and then go home.

The next evening Blossom had an evening Tupperware party to go to which turned out to be seventy-two dollars and eight cents with only nine people to attend. On the following Tuesday she felt energetic enough to make a mince meat pie and tarts, Jello and a lemon pudding. Wesley arrived home by seven-o'clock that evening, then by seven-thirty she had to be way across town for another Tupperware party, there was ten people attending, but only five ladies bought any Tupperware, the rest only came for the free gifts that were handed out.

Blossom arrived home by eleven-thirty and made Wesley's lunch for the next morning, and then she went to bed herself. Next morning Blossom woke up by Wesley and the kids, after he had left for work she brought the children back to bed with her for awhile. Blossom thought she would treat the children out that day, since it was such a beautiful day. She made their lunch and let them eat it out on the porch while playing house. After lunch was all finished Blossom got busy and made ten different pies then froze them all, then checked the mail to find that there was an invitation to Wesley's cousin's wedding to be held in the fall. At that moment Wesley arrived in the yard with a bouquet of flowers for her hidden behind his back, after he had washed up and shaved they all sat down at the supper table, then after supper a man from the life insurance company came over to try and sell Wesley some life insurance. Wesley and Blossom listened very carefully and then talked it through very carefully for awhile. Then decided that it was going to be a very good investment for the family, Blossom agreed, so Wesley signed on the dotted line for a fifty thousand dollar life insurance policy.

Blossom thought that if she still had her illness, then she more than likely would have been a high risk for a life insurance. The next day being a Friday, Blossom wasn't feeling too well, she had a terrific headache and then she started throwing up all over the place, as well as having stomach cramps, so she spent the entire afternoon in bed. Blossom had been working quite hard in the past four years trying to put her husband through trade school. After those long four years of selling Tupperware and constantly having to be on the phone for bookings, Wesley graduated from construction trade school, then they were doing much better and didn't have to have Blossom to work so hard so that they could scrimp to make ends meet. They were still living in the same older style house, and Bonny was getting to the age where she could soon start play school. Blossom was finding more time on her hands that she didn't know what to do with, so she started knitting slippers and sweaters for the children.

She still had her allergy from the pollen and she would get very sick with bad headaches in the spring, Wesley had to try and remember not to bring in any flowers to the house for her or she would end up very sick in a few days, but she managed to do quite well with her knitting and now that Wesley was back working full time, things got better for them.

Chapter Thirteen

Hard Times

April Fools day, the terrible fall Blossom had taken that last Sunday on the front steps while walking down from the entrance of the church, in which they had spent their morning praying, It was still bothering her lower part of her back. She had been dizzy that afternoon, after taking two of Wesley's pain killer pills, that was prescribed for his bad back he had hurt in a car accident awhile ago. When Blossom finally had the chance to lie down for awhile, she slept for four hours, only to awake to the pleasant sounds of Wesley playing with the children.

Blossom was feeling much better when she awoke, so she got up and dressed to go out, then dressed Bonny and Darcy to go out shopping. After all the groceries shopping were done, Bonny, Darcy and Blossom arrived home having to put the groceries away, Bonny decided to help her mummy. Blossom started dinner before Wesley would be finished work; he was getting a ride home with one of his co-workers that evening.

After dinner was ready and set on the table, she sat down to make out her work report to have ready for the Monday meeting. You see if the report wasn't ready for the Monday meeting, then the order in which she had to pick up for the following meeting would be late.

Monday morning bright and early Blossom drove Wesley to the construction sight across town to work and the children to the baby sitters. In order for Blossom to have the car that morning for Blossom's meeting, on the other side of town. By nine A.M. the meeting had gotten under way. There wasn't much new business that morning. So by 11:55 am she was on her way back to the warehouse to pick up her order for deliveries that needed to be made up that week. By the time she reached the intersection her car had gone out of control,

Blossom ended up on the opposite side of the road on the sidewalk, between a telephone pole and the highway. She never told her parents so not to get them worried. After stopping the Toyota and finally been able to see what had happened to put her car out of control she fell sick to her stomach. Blossom remembers Mrs. Bailey calling out to her while she was still in a daze. Blossom was still sitting behind the steering wheel in the car with no broken bones, but shook up a lot. There were people staring all around at her as if she was a caged animal in a zoo. Blossom heard Mrs. Bailey call out to her, "Blossom Honey are you all right?" That was the first time her mother-in-law called her Honey," No one ever called Blossom Honey except Wesley before. Mrs. Bailey had a real concern look on her face, she told all the lookers to go home or some place else and that this wasn't any freak show to watch. Mrs. Bailey stayed by Blossom's side the whole time and only left her long enough to make a couple of phone calls at the corner store to the police and tow truck, as Blossom couldn't drive the car after that. Blossom was thinking about what the people would of thought if they knew she use to have Petit-Mal, because there is a very few percentage of people who ever really out grow petit-mal. There had been something wrong with the steering after she ended up on the side walk, Not that she wanted to drive way across town anyway to get home, she was too shaken up from the whole ordeal. By now she was able to get out of the car; she had never been in any kind of a car accident before, where she was behind the wheel. By this time she was just shaken like a leaf in the breeze. She was escorted over to the police car an opposite side of the busy highway to make out a report of the accident. Lucky for Blossom there weren't any cars coming as she was still in a bit of a daze from the whole ordeal. Before she had to fill the accident report out, one of the police officer's took out his tape measure to measure the skid marks from her car in the intersection, Blossom found out later that would determine on how fast she was traveling. Blossom was doing speed limit, in fact she might have been going slower than the speed limit, since she slowed down before approaching the intersection. Blossom has always been leery about busy intersections. The steering had something to do with the front wheel. Blossom figured that she must have banged it on the telephone pole before bringing her car to a complete stop. The telephone pole was standing up straight then, she said a quiet little prayer for the safety of herself and any one else that might of been involved. This Toyota was an automatic car and when she brought the car to a stop, it just died out on its own, right there on the sidewalk facing the opposite way, she had been traveling before the tow truck man would take the car away, he first had to have a deposit for towing the car, he then took Blossom's name and address as well as her telephone number, and then Blossom gave him the deposit for towing the car away.

Mrs. Bailey new how shaken up Blossom was; as they were traveling to the warehouse in her manager station wagon, brown and white, to pick up both of their orders for the following week to be delivered. They loaded their orders up in the back end of her Ford wagon that Mrs. Bailey had won as a manager.

    Blossom thought that if she still had her petit-mal she would have constantly been blacking out all afternoon, so she was glad to be rid of it and have her mother-in-law there too. You see Mrs. Bailey was her manager as well as her mother-in-law and all managers received a Ford station wagon, all power, but when they step down from a manager's position that meant that they had to give the car back to the company. So Blossom was so grateful for her mother-in-law to be her manager, she didn't live too far from her either, so she wouldn't be going out of her way taking Blossom home that afternoon. First Mrs. Bailey had to make a stop on her way home to drop off some back orders to one of her customers. Blossom stayed in the car. Mrs. Bailey did the drop off first since her customers just lived not far from the warehouse. Blossom was still quite upset about the car and didn't want Wesley to find out about getting their only means of transportation out of commission from anyone else, until she could figure out how to tell him herself. While Mrs. Bailey was in the customer's house she asked to use the phone to phone Wesley, Wesley was at home at the time still busy baby sitting their two children. She told Wesley the whole story, but asked him not to worry that Blossom was all right and she would be bringing Blossom home soon, as a mother she also told Wesley not to come too hard down on Blossom. Soon Mrs. Bailey and Blossom was back on their way home. Blossom still was quite upset and not knowing how Wesley would take it, as she didn't know that Mrs. Bailey had phoned Wesley first. Wesley ended up getting worried anyway after he had hung up the phone, from talking to his mother, He then decided to phone Jan and asked if she wouldn't mind coming over to sit with the children. Jan was Wesley's sister-n-law, Wesley had explained what had happened and then waited for her to come before he started out the door; hitch hiking down the road to where he thought his mother and wife would be. Only to find he had missed them and had to hitch hike all the way back home again, a wasted trip he thought to himself. Jan was really good with the children and Bonny and Darcy really liked having her there. It wasn't too long after that Blossom had arrived home and Mrs. Bailey helped unload the wagon with her orders. Mrs. Bailey hadn't had much success in trying to calm Blossom down on the way home. Blossom nerves were quite a bit on edge even then. When Blossom had finally settled down in the house, Jan made her a cup of tea and told her to go lay down on the bed for awhile, she would stay with the children until Wesley had arrived back home. In an hour Wesley arrived home and Jan went home to tend to her family. Wesley was still very worried about Blossom then. On the following morning after Blossom was having a very sleepless night. They both hitch hiked down across town over the bridge to the garage where the car was still sitting. Blossom had a Tupperware party to attend that evening, since she knew she couldn't possibly get to it without any wheels, she really wasn't up to facing a lot of people that evening anyway, after what had just happened. Blossom decided to give away the Tupperware party to her mother-in-law to do and then when she would be able to sell again her mother-in-law could give her one of hers in return. That was what you call the buddy system Wesley took Blossom to the police station hitch hiked all the way to find out the name and address of the police officer who had attended the accident the morning before, when they arrived there they found out that the officer at the desk wouldn't give out that information. Blossom was still quite quiet about the whole matter, they then hitch hiked in town to see the car insurance people. Jan had been staying with the children again while Blossom and Wesley were busy in town. At one point Wesley had been walking backwards behind Blossom, he had stopped walking right in Blossom's path without letting her know and she of course didn't realize it until her hitch hiking thumb entered into his opened mouth. In a loving fashion Wrestle bit it and shocked her right out of her tree Blossom had never hitch hiked before and she figured that with all the hitch hiking they had done that she would be able to have a good nights sleep. On the following day Blossom was sure stiff from all that walking, she wasn't use to it like Wesley was. Wesley managed to find enough money to have the car towed back across the bridge to their home, where he could do his own repair on it and save the cost of labor charges by someone else. Wesley had found out that the brakes had sprung and that was why Blossom couldn't drive the car. In the past he had done most of his own car repairs. Blossom wasn't too eager to drive again after that accident. Wesley was able to tighten up the brakes so he could drive it in order to get back to work the next morning. Wesley had been so good about the whole mess Blossom had gotten herself into, never yelled at her once about the cost of repairs, and that time things were quite hard then to make ends meet. Blossom was up early the next morning with the children; Darcy had been teething that week, after awhile they all went for a walk in the sunshine. Blossom fed her children lunch after their long walk in the sunshine, and then did her usual order phoning. Wesley had all ready left the house early that morning for work, or at least she had thought that he had, until he came home early that afternoon and had explained to her what had happened that morning at the construction site Apparently Wesley arrived that morning to work and no one else showed up, he decided to leave and go find another job, one that was more reliable. He managed to find another construction site job that he could start first thing Monday morning.

    Come Friday evening Wesley and Blossom got all dressed up and then got the children dressed up to stay at their grandparents place while they were at Wesley's high school reunion party. The reunion was all right, Blossom had never been at a reunion before, but after awhile the party got rather dull, so they both left and Wesley took Blossom for a Chinese dinner.

Monday morning Wesley left the house bright and early to start his new job. Blossom got a ride with her mother-in-law to the Tupperware meeting again, only after the children were dropped off at Jan's. In the morning meeting they found out that the merchandise was going up in price, which meant that the dealers were getting a raise. That week Blossom worked harder than ever to sell the merchandise to help pay for the damage she had done to the car, the following Monday morning Mrs. Bailey didn't go into the meeting, she didn't tell Blossom until she had reached her home, which was a few miles away, that meant that she was to be responsible for those orders now. That was the first time Blossom had drove into town by herself since the accident, by which now was at least three months later, that morning she was being so careful thinking only of her driving as she had not realized that she had forgotten her cheque for her own order at home, (you see they only accepted certified cheques, and only after you had given the cheque, were you able to pick up your order.

In the evening Blossom told Wesley what had happened that morning, so right away after supper they dressed up the children and went out to the warehouse across the bridge in town to pick up the order and bring them their cheque before closing time. That way she could pick up her order and have packed and delivered it on time. Once Blossom had picked up her order, she still had to bag them into individual orders. Blossom had been haunted with those terrible headaches again. On the following day it was one of those days when you should have stayed in bed," To start off with, Blossom never got enough sleep the night before, in the morning it started off by her still feeling quite tired, the children were into more trouble than usual that afternoon, fighting with each other. Wesley never arrived home from work on time, in fact he never arrived home until eight-thirty that evening and didn't even have the courteous to phone and let her know that he was working late. Blossom was rushing around the house to feed the children and get them all ready for bed, as well as getting herself ready for her job that evening, which was to be at eight P.M.

The job then only turned out to be a sale of thirty dollars with two hours work, After traveling way across town and only to find nine people to turn up, Blossom was a little unhappy and only stayed long enough to collect the orders, she didn't even bother to stay for tea, Blossom was home by ten-thirty only to find everyone including Wesley, were fast asleep in their beds.

On Friday, it turned out to be a Friday the thirteenth and it sure tried hard enough to be miserable, just like a Friday the thirteenth would be if you were superstitious. Wesley arrived home by six that evening after putting in a full days work out on the wet construction site, only to say that he had been laid off, then Blossom had supper on the table which had been late too, it wasn't ready to eat until seven-thirty. After a bit they put Bonny and Darcy down to sleep, then by ten Wesley had gone to sleep too. That was when Blossom had discovered that Bonny had wet on the arm chair in the living room earlier, she had thought that by now Bonny had out grown wetting herself The following morning Wesley cleaned out the septic tank out back, while Blossom did some more phoning for orders, she knew that now it was up to her to support the family with Wesley out of work and all those bills had to be paid, so Blossom worked harder than ever again with her orders. Around eleven in the morning they all decided to take the dog and the children and pack a picnic lunch, then just take off to the lake to get some fishing in, Wesley had always liked to fish, it seemed to relax him, it was nice leaving all the troubles behind them that day. Blossom's headaches had gone away only for awhile too. Wesley was humming while the kids were listening to the birds singing their summer songs in the sunshine, driving along the lakeside looking for a good fishing hole to stop at.

The next day Wesley went down to the manpower building and then out to a construction site, to see if they were hiring any men on, in which he had struck it lucky and he was able to start work bright and early the next morning.

After dinner Wesley got busy and varnished the china cabinet he was making for their fourth anniversary, it was looking good by then. Wesley noticed that Blossom was starting to put on a little weight around her middle and kidded her about it, Blossom decided to go on a strict diet. In which she was hoping to loose fifty pounds by July, that was when the dealers and their managers were heading out to the Jubilee for a week out West, they have the Jubilee every year in some place out of province, but you have to qualify to and Blossom did this time. Blossom was really hoping that she had enough willpower to be able to stay away from sweets until then, that was her down fall, she loved sweets.

On April the nineteenth Blossom found out that Wesley wouldn't be getting aid for the following good Friday, they had hoped that he would, since they had planned on leaving around seven-thirty in the morning to go to the lake again, only that time his mother had offered to keep the children for the day while Wesley and Blossom were up at the lake by themselves. By April thirty-first Blossom had gone off her diet and she was getting worried, since she hadn't started her periods as of then, she had been feeling fairly tired the last couple of days.

That evening after the children had a story read to them and tucked into bed just down the hallway, Wesley and Blossom got out the coloring equipment to color the Easter eggs, then by the morning all the colored eggs would be out on the kitchen table in a wicker basket for a surprise for when Bonny and Darcy woke up. Happy Easter everyone, by ten that morning they were all dressed and had their Easter eggs and juice for breakfast, ready to go to church.

In town that day there was a fair going on that afternoon, so after church Wesley took his family out to see the country fair, Bonny and Darcy like the pony rides the best, then off to the Cartwright's where they played a couple of games of pool before dinner. That evening after having a good time with Blossom's parents they came home and put the very sleepy children down to bed, then went to bed themselves, only not to sleep, if you know what I mean, Blossom voice went quiet when she said it Wesley was in a very romantic mood that evening, Blossom on the other hand was in a bit of a romantic mood herself, they made passionate love until day break.

The very next morning Wesley noticed after they were able to pull themselves out of bed that Blossom wasn't feeling too well again, he just thought about the situation and chalked it up to a very late night, but she wasn't able to hold down any food in the morning. Blossom had managed to get out some bookings for in May and then pack the orders on the small living-room floor; there wasn't any place to walk through. She also managed to get two loads of the children's laundry done and, made supper. Bonny and Darcy colds seamed to be getting much better, but now Blossom figured that she was catching the same cold too.

Blossom really liked her work as a sales representative for the organization she was working for, but those last few days she was wishing that she had never seen another party as long as she lived. Blossom wasn't feeling up to her parties those days. When Tuesday rolled around, she said that it must of been one of the most tiring days she had yet, to start off with she never got too much sleep again and had terrible tension headaches, that evening her cold kept her awake most of the night, then Wesley had the same cold that everyone else had come down with.

Blossom woke up at seven-thirty with Bonny and little Darcy then she never got back to sleep that morning at all. In the afternoon they did manage to get about two hours shut eye, before it was time to make dinner and then get ready for her party that evening. After dinner she left the house for the Tupperware party after kissing Wesley and the children good-bye to go across town again. Blossom had arrived right on time, in fact she waited for an hour in her car, in the driveway and it was cold outside of her hostess's home just to find out that the hostess had forgotten about the party and had gone out for the evening. Blossom didn't want to wait in the house with the husband and son, since she noticed they had been drinking beer, they both were only wearing their shorts and a T shirt when the husband opened the door to her.

After one hour in the car in the dark of night, Blossom finally went home very disturbed at the whole ordeal. She was home by nine that evening, madder than a wet hen, When Blossom got mad, her Irish temper really showed through, She had promised herself earlier that the very next morning she was going to phone that darn women and give her a pierce of her mind. She did just that. Well! did she ever phone that women, apparently the so called lady had changed her mind about having the party, but didn't bother to let Blossom know, instead she let Blossom come expecting a Tupperware party and having to end up waiting in the cold of the night.

After a bit the kids got on her nerves so bad that she had thought that she was going to have a nervous break down, course Wesley was at work when it all happened, so he never knew what she had been going through that day. It was the same old routine on the following Thursday with her bookings, doing the laundry and feeding the children, she had that routine for so long that by now she was getting damn fed up with it, in fact if Blossom hadn't had her job to get out of the house sometimes she would go straight up a tree and back down again some days.

Blossom had wished that Wesley would take notice sometimes and help her out when she wasn't feeling up to it, but he never did. Friday everything was going real fine, she even painted the bathroom walls that afternoon, Then when Wesley came home she gave him his mail from the insurance company and that was when it happened, Wesley and Blossom had a fight of the century and he left in the car real upset. It wasn't until much later that Blossom had discovered that Wesley's pain killer pills were missing from the medicine cabinet in the bathroom. That made Blossom really worry about him, you see long before they were married Wesley had tried to commit suicide by taking an over dose of sleeping pills, now Blossom still worries about him, deep down in her heart she knew that Wesley wouldn't ever do it again. By then it was ten in the evening and he still hadn't been home, Blossom was beginning to really get worried, so she phoned his parents and then her sister in town, Cynthia, she had seen Wesley earlier that evening, but didn't know where he was now, his parents hadn't heard from him either. Blossom was trying very hard not to let the children see her worried look on her face.

She had wished that he would come home and then she knelt down beside the couch and prayed for his safety, Blossom prayed like she had never prayed before to the good Lord above. The worrying was really getting to Blossom and now her tension headaches started in on her again too. Blossom finally sat down to try and calm down before she might wake up Bonny and Darcy. She kept repeating the whisper, "GOD YOU KNOW I LOVE HIM," over and over to herself

Finally Wesley arrived home in the wee hours of the morning, when he entered the house through the front door, he found Blossom lying on the couch crying her eyes out. Wesley apologized and then they went to bed, the next morning they decided to deliver her orders together, after that onto the bank and by three Blossom had her doctor's appointment, she needed a note from her doctor saying it was OK to join the T.O.P.S CLUB (TOPS means take off pounds sensibly That was what Blossom wanted to do, none of those fast diets worked on her, she didn't believe in them anyway. So Blossom figured that maybe since she couldn't loose weight by herself, maybe they could help her loose the excess pounds.

Wesley then treated them all out to a chicken dinner, to try to make up for some of the pain he had caused her the night before. "He really was a wonderful man," Blossom would say with a smile across her face as big as Texas, then her smile faded away when she remembered that sometimes he just didn't feel as though he was a good father and husband as he thought they had expected of him, but Blossom wanted him to be just himself. When ever he thought that way he would get very depressed and start a fight so he could have a reason for leaving the house for awhile.

After Wesley had dropped Blossom and the kids off at home again, he left to see about a sideline job, to try and help out with the bills a little better, he was home again and in bed beside Blossom by ten-thirty P.M. You see they might go out for an occasional dinner, but they never squandered their money and most of the time their bills were paid up to date. Blossom went right off to sleep as soon as she heard that her man was home safe.

On the following Sunday after church they took Bonny and Darcy to the park to play in for awhile, Wesley and Blossom sat on the luscious green grass watching them play on the swings and slide, laughing as they play, then off to his parents home again, that was so Wesley could see his dad and ask him for some help with his car to fix the carburetor, they ended up staying for dinner which Blossom helped his mother prepare and then clean up later.

On Monday it was a funny sort of a day, to start off with Blossom went to her meeting with Mrs. Bailey, she made sure that she hadn't forgotten her cheque that time. When Blossom finally went to the warehouse to pick up her order, she had found out that they weren't in as of yet, they wouldn't be in until May seven either. Wesley was still having trouble with his car, so he had decided to take the car into garage to be fixed properly, they loaned him a courtesy car to use in the mean time. By dinner time Wesley came home with a big surprise, he had apparently bought himself a motorcycle, it was a second hand one, a trail bike, "I think." Blossom was surprised all right, that it even started up, since the fellow who sold it to him, wouldn't let him take the bike out on the street to try it out first. He after all was afraid that Wesley wouldn't come back with the bike that was what he had told her, with a smile beaming back from ear to ear on his face.

After what had seamed like a long time of convincing Blossom that the bike was a going to save them money in the long run, Wesley took them all out in the car for supper, that evening he phoned his brother Rod right away, only Jan answered and hung up on him not realizing who it was.

The following day was when Blossom's brand new harvest gold stove was arriving. Wesley had put a down payment on it awhile ago, now he was able to pay the whole thing off, the old white stove that was left with the house only had one burner working and the oven didn't work at all. That same afternoon Mrs. Bailey came over for a visit, and then Blossom froze some rhubarb and cleaned out the twenty-three cubic deep freezer in her kitchen. Around five-thirty Wesley and Casey surprised her and brought the new stove home themselves, Casey helped Wesley carry it into the kitchen through the living room, they looked at

Wesley's new motorcycle and then he left for home where his supper was waiting for him there. After Blossom having the honor of making a delicious supper on her new stove, she then left to do her grocery shopping, while Wesley had the children to look after and the dishes to clean up, after the children ended up helping him fix his bike in the front driveway. By the time that Blossom had arrived home with her arms loaded down with groceries, Wesley had the brain wave to spread a large sheet of news paper and cardboard on the kitchen table, in order for him to work on his motorcycle parts which had been spread all over the kitchen table. Westley's hands were just filled with grease and Blossom didn't know where she was going to put all the groceries in the kitchen, with his motorcycle parts spread all over, she could of killed him on the spot; as Blossom was telling me this; remembering back when she had the sound of a scolding voice in her tone.

On May fourth they got up and in the time Blossom went to turn on the heat in the house, she discovered that they had no heat at all. So Blossom got on the phone and phoned the oil company, since Wesley was at work, she had purchased thirty-five dollars worth of oil for their furnace, the furnace was set up in the garage, after he had finished filling up the tank, she then discovered that the furnace wouldn't start. In the mean time the kids had to keep warm with their colds, All Blossom could think of was how to keep the children warm, She then lit the fire in the fire place and let them sit around the fire wrapped in heavy blankets in the middle of the living room, this happened when it was a cold spell in May. Later in that same afternoon a sales man came over to sell her a genuine cowhide with gold engraving on the cover of a brown album, it was one of those gimmicks where you buy the photo album now, the cost was ninety-nine dollars, then for the next six years you can be able to get any eight by ten colored portraits done of the family free, you see in the ninety-nine dollars you were paying for it all. Blossom decided to get it and wrap it up for Wesley's father's day present. In the late afternoon Wesley went down to his father's home to work on his motorcycle, while they were down there Darcy and Blossom went to the department store, Bonny wanted to stay with her father, she was getting more and more like a Tomboy every day, she liked to work around cars and climb trees, you know the type.

Next morning Wesley was up and gone to work before Blossom was even awake. It was the same old routine for her and the children, doing the ironing and laundry, then getting on the phone to try and get a few more bookings up for the following week. The following Monday the new dealers gifts that the hostess could win by selling one hundred dollars in sales and having two other people at their party book a party with in thirty days, it was the new chase lounge in a beautiful yellow floral print and orange edging. That afternoon Blossom had to pick up Wesley from work, since she had the car that morning and he couldn't bring his tools on the motorcycle, so on the way home from picking up Wesley they let the children play at the park again for awhile, then left for home In the evening Blossom mentioned, she must really be tired from the events of the day since she had just snapped at Wesley for no reason. By May eighth it was very cold, and it looked as though there was a storm coming up in the north.

On the following Wednesday Blossom was very busy phoning lumber yards for Wesley about price lists on some plywood for his work, by that time he was working on his own, finishing a basement in town. After Blossom had finished getting all the prices lists for him, she then did up the breakfast dishes and made the beds, washed and waxed the floors, then did up a load of laundry, by the time she was finished it was time for Wesley to return home again, just as he was entering through the front door, Blossom was decorating a large chocolate cake that she had made for Mother's day, she had picked out green icing with a mint flavoring. As soon as the cake was finished she had scrambled some eggs for supper and Wesley worked on the china cabinet in the living room, after awhile he was busy building another part of the china cabinet for Blossom for mother's day, Blossom finished up the dishes and strolled over to Wesley to give him a peck on the cheek, then went to wash and set her long blonde hair, by ten-thirty they were all tucked snug in bed once again.

The very next morning Blossom did the usual things a wife and mother of two usually does, for supper she had decided to make Wesley rolled brisket with corn on the cob and mashed potatoes, his favorite, that same evening she joined the T.O.P.S. club, it was a club for over weight people and it taught you how to take off pound sensible after being weighed in, which was very embarrassing for Blossom, then attending the club for two weeks straight she had lost one and half pounds.

In those days she was having those terrible headaches that took the place of her Petit-mal, she was hoping to find someway to get rid of them for once and for all.

Blossom went to visit her sister Willette at work and then came straight home, only to find that Wesley had changed the whole living room around, By eleven-thirty he decided to let Blossom know that he was looking for some passionate love making from her, only to find this time he was to find out that she was the one that was too tired for any horsing around, but he carried it through even though she was not willing.

On Friday May eleventh, Blossom had another very busy day a head of her, to start off with she did up three loads of dirty laundry, cut the front lawn with the old push lawn mower that just didn't want to keep going, instead it would stall out, then the children and herself all went for a long walk down the road to mail a very important letter, then came home for lunch, put the children down for their afternoon naps, and then moved the pole lamp that her parents had given them for a gift, to a better spot. After that Blossom decided to take a rolled news paper and start killing some ants one-hundred in and out of her house, some on the back porch, the big carpenter ants, "you know the type," Blossom would say. Wesley was late coming home that evening, so they ended up eating their meal late again, "if there ever was a time that, that man of mine wasn't late for dinner I don't know when," Blossom would say in a voice that sounds like she was remembering the way it use to be. While she was waiting for Wesley to arrive home, Blossom took the turkey out of the freezer to thaw, then washed and waxed some floors, by ten the new china cabinet was all finished except for the gold pebble like surface glass doors, the ones she wanted to put in, but couldn't afford at the time, they managed to change the new china cabinet for the old book case, "You see Blossom had managed to save little by little to buy her china set before they were married, and that china set was to be used only on special occasions. Mrs. Bailey came over the following morning to help Blossom with her turkey for the first time. Finally the day arrived when Blossom was feeling more run down every day and when one evening when Wesley didn't come home until seven-thirty and her dealer's meeting was held at seven-thirty at her managers home, which was about twenty miles away, she was late.

By June the first it was one of those days again, Blossom remembers as she looks through their old photo album sitting on the front porch, she finally said that everything went wrong that afternoon, to start with that was the day that Wesley couldn't get time off work to get his permit, his customer didn't have the blue prints ready and they got a bill in the mail for forty-three dollars, it should of read thirty-five dollars from the oil company, there was a eight dollar and fifty cents charge for court costs in which they hadn't had the slightest knowledge about at the time. Then off they went again out doing their weekly grocery shopping.

Blossom always felt better after she did some shopping. That evening when they were back with their groceries and two very tired children, they had discovered that only half of the groceries they had purchased were there. Wesley quickly phoned the grocery store, since they were only opened for a few minute longer, the next morning they all went back to where they received their furnace oil, spoke to person in charge and straightened up that mess. By nine-thirty that same morning they finally received the rest of their groceries. Wesley then took his family and bought a small playpen type fence to keep the children off the road.

Monday at the meeting Blossom won a forty-five dollar set of dinnerware in a pretty blue pattern, then one-hundred-sixty calendar cards to be handed out at her parties, which otherwise she would of had to pay for them, also received her coffee set that she had been so patiently waiting for some time now, then at four in the afternoon Blossom went to see her doctor in town and he wanted to take a pregnancy test from her for that coming Thursday the seventh at two in the afternoon. Blossom picked up Wesley after the doctors appointment and told him what the doctor had suspected with her that she might be pregnant again.

It was two and half years since Darcy, Wesley was full of smiles from ear to ear that afternoon with just the thought that he might be a new daddy again, In fact he wouldn't even let Blossom make dinner that evening.

The very next week it was much the same old routine, as they were waiting patiently for the day to come when they would find out if the rabbit had died or not. Then came the seventh and it was the time for Blossom to go to see the doctor again. What a busy afternoon it turned out to be, Bonny and Darcy helped her to hurry to be ready by twelve noon for Wesley to pick them all up, but Wesley didn't get home until one in the afternoon. Then on the way taking Blossom to the doctors he had to first drop the children off at the baby sitters.

After that he went on his way, by three in the afternoon Wesley had picked Blossom up again at the doctors office after traveling way across town that early afternoon, Blossom had showed negative to the rabbit test.

The following day she got another outside booking for her job and twenty-five dollar sale to boot just over the phone. Wesley didn't work that day after all, instead he got a lot of his running around done for the job, you know the last minute details. He was able to pick up the permit from city hall that afternoon. Wesley came home at about two in the afternoon, then at three thirty they all went out and got some strawberries from Blossom's mother, she had about three and half acres in which she grew and sold them to the public. After dinner Wesley worked on his motorcycle again, his pride and joy, Blossom did the dishes and two loads of very dirty children's laundry, then she put the children off to sleep after telling them a bed time story, baked a cake in the evening.

What a rushed week, the very next week turned out to be just like the first one. Blossom had one party and two bookings, sold over one-hundred thirty dollars and forty cents. Wesley went to work on Saturday afternoon, something he usually didn't do. In the morning of the next working day they decided to deliver the orders and Cartwright's moved into their new Spanish home, that Casey built and designed himself, On the piece of land where Blossom and Wesley had been renting the old house until they were able to find the place they are in now, this was about a year after they moved out, since then the bull dozer had come in and pushed down the old house where they now have the Spanish home

That evening Bonny and Blossom went into town and Wesley made dinner, then after dinner they all went out to his parent's home, so he could work on his motorcycle again with his dad. in the same evening when they finally arrived home and had put the children down to sleep. Wesley and Blossom retired to their bedroom with the door shut tight, so not to disturb the children while making love again all night long, while Wesley was making love to Blossom, he had a big sheepish look come across his radiant face, when! he said "I am really looking forward in having another child'" that was if Blossom was pregnant, so far the test showed that it was negative, Blossom was a little scared to have another child after the trouble she had giving birth to Darcy, but she never let on to Wesley that she was scared. Come Monday Blossom was feeling tired all day, at the assembly she forgot a box of merchandise, then gave a fellow worker a ride home and in return she gave Blossom ten egg separators for giving out at her Tupperware parties. Blossom then left to pick up Wesley and stopped in at her mother's to pick up the beautiful doll she had hidden away for Bonny's birthday, plus some material for herself that was given to her.

After dinner she made a skirt for Bonny out of the material, then did some embroider on it, Wesley went back to work in town after dinner and never arrived back home until ten-thirty very, very tired too.

June twelfth Darcy's second birthday, Blossom made a birthday cake and did up the house work in an hour, she washed down the hallway and bathroom floors. She also managed to get some ironing done up. Then got her quilt down to work on, Blossom had started that quilt ever since Bonny was born, she hadn't worked on it for a couple of months now, it was a patch work quilt that was made out of an old white bed sheet and left over material and worn out clothing, very colorful.

That same evening they were suppose to get their first portraits done from the album she had purchased for father's day before, Blossom had bought Wesley, I told you about earlier in this book, but Blossom forgot the certificate at home, so by the time they finally had arrived at the studio they were too late for the appointment, Wesley was just furious with Blossom then.

That same evening blossom had a T.O.P.S meeting around seven-thirty, it was the same time that the portraits were to be taken, so she left with the baby shower present she had purchased that same week earlier, this was for another girl who just had a pretty baby girl one week prior. Around nine-thirty Mom Bailey brought over Darcy's birthday present and after she had left, they all went to bed very tired, but not before taking lots of pictures of Darcy on his second birthday.

The very next morning Blossom figured that she had the touch of the flu that was going around, at least after dinner she had to practically live on the throne in the bathroom, Blossom was so sure that she was pregnant, since sometimes she could feel that there was life inside her. Blossom did her report for their Monday meeting and ever time she went to use the phone there was a very rude person that kept picking up the receiver on their party line, sometimes she couldn't get to use the phone until way in the late afternoon, because somebody's kids would be either on it or left the receiver off the hook. You see on that particular party line was about ten families and one family had about ten children. After what had seemed a long time they finally got a private line put in their home. "Blossom said, "It was worth every penny they had put out for that phone line.

Chapter Fourteen

Their Big Move

    The weeks passed and then month until the day came that Blossom would find out that she was right about being with child. She was getting bigger as the days passed by, Wesley was very excited, and he came home from work one afternoon beaming from ear to ear with the excitement of the good news.
    They shopped for tiny clothes that could do for either sex, Dawn gave them a second hand crib and baby buggy, Bonny's old chest of drawers will now be painted blue and white and fixed up for the new arrival. The sewing room will be made over for a baby's room in their tiny country home, yes as I recall there were a lot of preparations to be made before the big day, when the little bundle of joy arrived into this world of bewilderment.
    Blossom was still working as a sales rep. and running the house in the mean time. She kept Bonny's and Darcy's old diapers and diaper pail, which had kept her very busy those days cleaning out the diaper pails and sterilizing the flannel diapers. Blossom continues to stay with T.O.P.S. club, since they had what you call a stork club section for mothers to be, while losing the excess weight. The dealers in the sales job had gotten together and all had chipped in for a blue and sliver mesh playpen, It was a real treat to have a baby shower," since the first two children she hadn't any baby shower, "Oh don't get me wrong Blossom would go on saying," they brought many wonderful gifts up to her in the hospital room for Bonny and Darcy, but this was her very first baby shower.
    The months were getting closer to her time now; she was having a harder time to sleep. Their neighbors were all getting excited for Blossom too. There was just one month left to go before she was to give birth to their third child, Wesley and Blossom had been talking about Wesley actually taking part in the delivery, of his new born child, at this time the husbands were aloud to watch

the birth of their child, he wasn't aloud with their first two children, but at this time doctors were letting them come into the delivery room as long as they wore a white surgical gown and mask.

More and more fathers were taking the opportunity in doing so. Most fathers to be thought it was so great, first Wesley would be excited about seeing his child coming threw the doors of life, and then he would be having second thoughts on the whole matter, by now Blossom was having five minute pains coming, then they would stop, every evening her birth pains would start at 9 P.M. and end every night at midnight. In fact a couple of time Blossom ended up going into hospital on false labor, once in the middle of the afternoon when she was by herself with Bonny and Darcy and no transportation to get around, her water broke and she had to telephone her parents to come all the way across town to rush her to the hospital then back across town again, Casey took care of the children while Dawn took Blossom into the maternity ward three floors up. After the nurses on duty had prepared Blossom for delivery, it only turned out to be another false alarm again, this happened two or three times before she finally gave birth. When the day finally came, Wesley took her into the hospital around two in the afternoon; they prepped her and got Blossom signed into the maternity ward. Blossom was taking longer in the labor room than usual; they had her walk the floors for about one or two hours until it was virtuelly impossible to walk any longer.

Blossom didn't quit remember the exact amount of time, but it was getting harder and harder for her to walk the floors, Wesley was right beside her all the way helping her when it got too hard to stand, let alone walk anymore. Finally after Wesley was helping Blossom to do her prenatal breathing in the labor room, the labor pains would come on stronger and closer together. By that time the doctor had decided to move her into the case room (or delivery room) which ever they called it at the time, at this point Wesley had put on a surgical gown and mask and then he was sent into the case room along with Blossom, since she was to be about another half hour before they thought she would be ready to deliver. Blossom had a doctor who was on call that afternoon, since her own doctor had finally gone on holidays; he had put off his holidays long enough waiting for Blossom to go into labor, but Blossom turned out to be fifteen days past due, so he took his holidays in hopes that she wouldn't be ready until he had gotten back.

That was why the doctor on call was taking over for Blossom's doctor's appointments, Blossom, couldn't remember the doctor's name it was so long ago, but he was a real caring person with a beard and mustache. Well at this point the doctor on call had decided to go down stairs to the cafeteria for a cup of coffee, while the nurses were in the middle of shift change, When! All of a sudden the baby was entering the birth canal. Well! Wesley just seen the head of his new born child appear through the birth canal from where he was standing at the head of the delivery table, he just looked straight down at Blossom's face filled with bewilderment by the sight he had just witnessed, but joy also of being able to be one of the few first fathers to witness the birth of his child. The look that Wesley had on his face was the kind of a look that only a mother to be can experience, that look was a look of rapture that was hard to explain, the feeling a women gets when she finally gives birth, is a feeling of gladness, meaning that you are glad that the pain is finally all over, but joyful too of knowing that this tiny little creature is apart of you and the one you love so dearly.

There also was that joyous feeling that you know that you have a healthy little bundle of joy to love and to hold and to nurse while bringing that baby into the world where there is so much hate and disorder to people's lives. A baby can mend all the hurts she's ever had just by being there to love. Finally the nurse rang the pager of the doctor, he didn't get a chance to have his cup of coffee, in which he had to run pretty fast back up the stairs to the third floor to help Blossom in the delivery room, at 4:28 that sunny afternoon the baby was finally born into the working world. The very first thing Wesley had said to Blossom as she remembers was that moment when he shouted out "It's a boy! A dark hairs middle age nurse with a big smile across her face looked at Wesley straight in the eye and said with a quiet voice back to him No! It's a girl, a ten pound five ounce bouncing baby girl, "As she had laid the baby girl on a clean pink towel across Blossom's chest. Blossom asked Wesley if he would like to hold his brand new baby daughter, but in a joking manner he said back, I'm not going to hold that slimy little thing, "Wesley and Blossom decided to name her April Lynn. After giving birth to April Lynn, Blossom was then put under general anesthetics in which she was still in the same case room. This surgery was for Blossom's cervix, it had to be sewn up in which April Lynn had torn open on her way out the doors of life. Blossom was in the case room for over an hour, when she finally came out of the anesthetic, the very first thing she did was want to phone her parents, she had been very close to her parents in the last few years, only to find out that Wesley had all ready phoned the good news to them as they had been anxious waiting for his call, Wesley had told them everything.

After coming out of the case room she was wheeled passed the nursery, which there was a large picture window that she could look at April Lynn from her hospital bed, at the window she could see her new baby girl. Still a little groggy from the anesthetic and still in her arm was the needle with the intervenes coming from the bottle was attached to the bed by a long steel rod; that hung over her head. She mumbled out that April Lynn looked like Jan, in which she hadn't looked like her at all, then onto the four bed ward where her bed was placed next to the washroom. In awhile the nurse came by with a bed pan and the very first thing Blossom said, I'll use the bathroom thank you," So the older nurse on duty at the time took the needle out from her arm that had the intervenes bottle attached to it so she could get up and use the bathroom, after that the needle stayed out. The bottle was attached by a clear tube like hose about one quarter in diameter which then hung from a stainless steel pole that had been attached to the head of the bed, after she had managed to get herself to the bathroom, Blossom came back to crank her hospital bed up at the foot end to a sitting position. The other new mothers in the ward were quite surprised on how fast Blossom had recovered after just having surgery from giving birth to a ten pound five ounce baby. They were amazed at the way she was since it was only half an hour since Blossom was still under the intervenes, after a bit, what had seemed to Blossom like a long time, the nurse then brought the babies around to the new mothers. Blossom couldn't wait until she could hold her bundle of joy; she was sitting up now so it was OK for her to have her baby too.

Wesley was in the room with her the whole time cueing over his baby, just as much as Blossom, they had to have the curtains drawn around them, so the mothers that were breast feeding the babies had privacy from the other fathers. Blossom and Wesley talked and for a awhile and then Blossom bent over to Wesley and gave him the sweatiest kiss she had ever gave him before.

Now it was feeding time again for the babies and the fathers were to either to go out in the waiting room down the hall or go home, or if they wished to they could pull the curtains shut again and be with their new family. Wesley decided to go home and be with Bonny and Darcy at that point, since he didn't want to take advantage of the Cartwright's good nature for too long, they were looking after the children again, with that in mind they said their good-bye's and he went on his way. As he was on his way to Grandma's house, he was remembering the cute way his new daughter was in the arms of his wife. A week had passed now, Blossom was ready to come home from the hospital, she had phoned Wesley that afternoon and there was no answer. The doctor wanted April Lynn to stay an extra day in the hospital because of her yellow Jaundice, (Jaundice is a symptom in which bilirubin a bile pigment is deposited in certain tissues of the body, giving the skin the mucus membrane, and the whites of the eyes a yellow color,) but Blossom said no!" She was not leaving the hospital without her baby again, she did with Darcy and that was pure hell. Blossom had gone through a lot of worrying back then, this time she talked to the doctor in letting her go home and bringing the baby back for a check up the next day, she continued to try and phone. Her parents were the next on the list thinking that Wesley might of been over there, only to find out that he wasn't so she asked her dad if he would please pick them up and take them home, but Casey and Dawn were headed out, and didn't want to be bothered with an unexpected drive out of their way. She was getting pretty anxious to find someone to bring them home, since she was some what depressed being in the hospital all day with nothing to do, her last chance was Mrs. Bailey and Blossom was running out of coins at the pay phone down the hall, in which there usually was an waiting line to get to the phone. Finally she got hold of Mrs. Bailey and she agreed to pick them both up and bring them both home.

By this time Blossom had made arrangements with the doctor to take April Lynn home that day. She was all ready to leave and was now dressing little April Lynn in her clothing of pink and white to bring her home. Blossom had purchased these clothes a month before she had April Lynn. Now April Lynn and Blossom were all ready, the cardboard box that the hospital gave the new mothers was all filled with flowers and gifts for April Lynn and Blossom which all her friends and family had brought to the hospital. The hospital also gave samples of disposable diapers, pabulum, canned milk, victims etc. which was also placed in the cardboard box. Now the time came for Blossom to go home, Mrs. Bailey had come up to the third floor to help Blossom to her station wagon parked out front, one nurse carried April Lynn, another carried the box of gifts and flowers, Mrs. Bailey carried some potted flowers and another nurse wheeled Blossom in a wheel chair to the car, they didn't let you walk to the car from the hospital in those days, when you come they wheel; you in and when you go, they wheel you out. After Blossom was in the front seat of the station wagon, the nurse carefully handed April Lynn to her to hold, while others put the flowers and gifts in the back of the station wagon. After what had seemed to be an awful long time for Blossom, she finally arrived home to see Wesley just pull into the driveway ahead of them, he had been at the paint store with Darcy and Bonny. Once April, Lynn was settled down in her crib in the master bedroom, Blossom came into the kitchen to find wooden carpenter horses and paint cans all over the place, she started to clean it up and the paint spilled all over the kitchen floor and stove. Blossom was so upset about the mess that Wesley just told her to lay down for awhile and he would clean it all up. Wesley could be so helpful for Blossom in that way, apparently he was going to surprise Blossom by wall-papering the baby's room, only to discover that the wall paper would not stay up, so he had gotten up tight with the whole matter that he just grabbed up the wallpaper that had fallen down off the walls and packed up the children to go to the paint store where there he put the crumbled wallpaper as well as the unused portions on the counter and demand his money back, the clerk told him that the store policy was to exchange, but no refunds, well! They tried to exchange the wall paper for other wall paper, but Wesley said no! Way," give me some paint then, that will work and that was what had happened while Blossom was trying to get hold of him while still in the hospital.

Wesley mentioned this to her after everything was cleaned and Blossom and April Lynn had a nice long rest after the trip home. The next day everything was back to normal, the baby's room had been freshly painted in a pale green and white, while Blossom was sleeping. Wesley was back at work again that day. She started back to work with house hold chores, and taking care of the three children now, then after a month or so she had decided to go back to work herself in sales. She managed to work it out so that the time she spent working Wesley was home with the children. You see they still needed the two incomes to live on.

The next Monday was the T.O.P.S. meeting and Blossom had a phone call late the night before to please bring April Lynn with her this time to the meeting. Blossom was able to loose seventeen pounds after having April Lynn, she was so proud of herself; the girls at T.O.P.S. had planned a baby shower for her that evening. They had given baby showers to the new mothers before in the club too. Since they had asked Blossom to bring April Lynn to the meeting this time, she figured something was up in the wind. Sure enough when she had arrived there that evening with April Lynn in the car bed, brought in by Wesley and set down on a long table so April Lynn could be admired by the other women in the club, she was right, they had planned a surprise baby shower for her. Everyone was there that evening all sitting around in the large rec-centre in a crescent shape on wooden chairs, most uncomfortable chairs around, one wooden chair was decorated for Blossom to sit on, while she was opening up all the lovely gifts for April Lynn, one of the ladies had asked Blossom if she may hold April Lynn on her lap, since April Lynn was awake, Blossom let her hold her, she had her most of the evening.

Blossom had received some real nice little frilly dressy outfits, bibs with the days of the week on, booties that had been knitted, diaper bag and diapers, dresses, all the things a new baby would need in the first months of her life. Blossom was so happy she new that they gave baby showers, but she never expected one for April Lynn. It always seemed to Blossom that when ever it was her turn for something that really mattered to Blossom like a baby shower or a house warming party, It seemed that things changed or something else was more important and Blossom would loose out. This time it was special, she had been given two baby showers one by T.O.P.S. and one by the sales personal from the girls who worked with her.

Well the time went by and things were getting harder as the time went on, Wesley was out of work now and the only income coming in was what Blossom would bring home, which wasn't very much, with his unemployment insurance and Blossom's income there wasn't very much left over at the end of the month for groceries and baby formula, since Blossom couldn't breast feed this time around, some how they managed with their good friends and families helping out when ever they could.

After about six months down the line Wesley was getting itchy feet and wanting to go out of province to look for work, his unemployment insurance was running out and the people that Blossom was selling to didn't have too much money either, those days, she wasn't bringing that much money home any more. The construction work had almost halted to a stop, Wesley had talked it over to his mother since his father was now in the hospital with cancer at the time, she thought it was a good idea for them to move out of province. Blossom how ever didn't want to move away from her family and friends, but she knew that her place was with her husband no matter what, and they had some real good arguments over the matter too. When the eighth month had come around, that was August, Wesley had just about made his mind up about leaving to look for work in Alberta, when his dad took a turn for the worst and this was a sorry time for all, every other day Wesley and Blossom would go up to see his dad in the hospital, they had moved him to Vancouver by this time. Now Blossom can recall that he was so afraid of a needle when the time came to give him pain killer by needle, because pills were not strong enough for his pain, Wesley had to hold his hand, Wesley sent for his younger brother Rod, to come out from Elcho B.C. since they figured that Mr. Bailey had very little time left to live. Rod came out the very next day and brought his family of two children with him, Mr. Bailey had just received a shot for his pain, he was in a lot of pain those days, when Wesley asked his dad if he knew Rod, his dad shaking his head as he couldn't speak any longer said no!, but yet he knew his grandchildren.

Mr. Bailey at that time couldn't use much of his reflexes, except to let you know by blinking of his eyes and the shaking of his head, Wesley and Blossom had talked it over about bringing Bonny, Darcy and little April Lynn up to the hospital to see him, but had decided not to, so that the children will remember him as he was, full of life, not as he is, on his death bed. A week later he was transferred back to the local hospital in which he had passed away a week or two later, Blossom couldn't quite remember the exact time. In the next few days Wesley had spent a lot of time with his mother trying to comfort her in her time of need, I guess she didn't really like me, "Blossom was saying, because when Blossom would try to comfort her she would just snap back at her and make Blossom felt like she wasn't welcomed into their family at all. One comfort thought Blossom had, was that at least he got to see his last grandchild before he had passed away. After the funeral services were over and his dad was in the ground to rest, Wesley had phoned his aunt and uncle in Alberta to see if he could come out and stay with them awhile, while looking for work out there. This was about one month later that he did this, Blossom was left behind with three children, no car to get around, no money to pay bills, and she had felt stranded, Oh! Her family would help out when they could, but it wasn't the same, anytime she had to go anywhere she had to bundle the three children up and put them in the little red wagon, and pull this wagon up and down the hills for groceries etc. Wesley would write and some of the letters were pretty bad ones too, Blossom would phone him and he would say no more phone calls, the cost was too much, he could see that she never phoned that often, only when she needed money for food and the children, because sometimes Blossom would go without a meal so that the children could have something to eat.

When Wesley had sent some money once, she had to use it on bills for the gas for the furnace and phone bill, utility bill etc. Blossom always got her bills paid up some how, when finally the family allowance cheque came in, which wasn't much back then, she used it for food. Wesley was gone for about two to three weeks when he wrote that he had a job out there and a place for them to stay, but they didn't allow dogs, which caused another argument in the family, because they had to give their little cok-a-poo away which was as much apart of the family as the children were, Now Blossom had to try and find someone that would maybe look after that dog until they had a place of their own, but nobody would help out, so she ended up giving that sweet little dog to her Aunt and Uncle. Blossom knew that it would be taken care of real well there and loved too, which was a big part of their family.

Finally the day came after a long waiting period of Wesley being away from his family for so long that they were ready to move to Alberta, it was Halloween and April Lynn was one year old now. In the late afternoon the family and friends came over to help load up their rented moving van, there was no room for the children's swing, so they decided to give it to Sheila's family for her little ones, her younger son was only about a year younger than April Lynn.

That evening they were invited to the Cartwright's for dinner with all the family present to say their good bye's, on the way out the little trick or theaters were all out with their bag goodies going from door to door, Dawn had given the children each some treats to munch on while traveling, since they would of missed the Halloween.

Just before they had arrived to the road that Sheila's home was on, one of the trick or treaters decided to throw an uncooked egg on the truck's window and on the door, what! a mess they had to stop at Sheila's to clean it all off before they could start on their way again, it was about eight o'clock when Wesley finally got his family on the way again with Bonny sitting up front in the middle, Darcy on Blossom's lap, by this time April Lynn was tired so she slept on the blanket on the floor at Blossom's feet near the heater keeping warm. This all happened in October of 1975 and it was cold out then. It was a long drive for them all, arriving to their destination in which they would be spending the night before going on again in the morning, everyone was so tired that they just didn't even try to get undressed, Wesley and Blossom just put the children down to sleep and when they were all settled in, then they went fast asleep too. The very next morning bright and early with the day crisp, the morning dew still on the ground and the sun still trying to peak through the dawning of the day, they had breakfast at a peak by truckers' restaurant where all the truckers usually stop. when making a Cal-Van run in the eighteen wheelers, after having breakfast and waking up they were on their way once again, singing and pointing out landscapes to the children, once in awhile getting out to stretch their legs and watch the children try and catch a small water fall on the side of the mountain, just to find out how cold the mountain water really is. Around about two in the late afternoon, they arrived at their new home in Alberta just to find that the house was all locked up and the people who lived down stairs of the upper duplex in the south end of town, these people had let Wesley use their phone to phone the landlord, they were very nice people, thought Blossom at the time, until she had gotten to know them better, but that was another story. Once the landlord had arrived and the doors were opened Wesley's uncle and cousins had arrived too, they were all ready to help unpack. now since they brought Blossom's golden stove out with them from B.C., it was a mother's day present, they didn't need the one in the kitchen, Blossom said it was so dirty anyway that she would of had to scrub that stove for a month of Sundays before she could even use it Well it turned out that the landlords didn't mind storing his stove in his garage, they moved Blossom's in for her then. Then came the 23 foot deep freeze loaded down with meat and frozen products that Blossom had frozen herself, in which the only place to put it was also in the kitchen, the kitchen was fairly large, but in order to get to it they had to bring them up the long flight of steps from the entrance out front, being that there was no back alley to drive the truck up to the back door, the snow was level with the back landing anyway. Wesley and his uncle had to bring all those about twenty steps straight up with no landing to take a rest on, Blossom had all ready empty the freezer and the food was in the kitchen in boxes waiting to go back into the freezer.

His uncle was a Husky man very strong, while Wesley had a bad back lifting those heavy appliances. The rest of the furniture was fairly easy to bring up the steps; there was no need of a fridge, since there was all ready one in place there. When the boxes of dishes came up, that was when Blossom took ever dish and cup one by one out and washed each one even the cutlery by hand and then dried each one, before putting them all away, this was weather or not they needed it, she didn't like the news print black marks on her dishes. Once moved in they began to grocery shop, now this was still in the middle of winter for Alberta, the snow was still on the ground and still very cold too. They had to bundle up the children pretty warm before going out again. The next day was a Sunday a day of rest and boy! Did they rest and then back to work for Wesley, Blossom became a full time mother and wife; no outside jobs for her, things were going pretty smoothly this time in their lives. Blossom still missed her family and would write quite a number of times to them. She didn't like to live that far away from her family, but she was trying for Wesley's sake, since she loved him very much and their three children, Blossom was very happy that she had no more petit-mal spells from her early days.

After awhile it got easier to be away from her mother and father for so long, she loved them very dearly, she felt a great pressure had lifted from her shoulders with that move and Wesley had said the same thing had happened to him.

You know Mrs. Bailey was always interfering in their family and that put a lot of pressure on them. Things were all right between them now, they were living quite happy, Dawn and Casey finally sold the house for them back in B.C. Wesley and Blossom were planning on another move to their own home again with a large fenced back yard for the children. Blossom said that things couldn't have been better out there for Wesley was still working and making good money in construction work, the most money he had ever made before.

Just before Blossom had fallen asleep on the porch in her rocking chair for the last time, she had mentioned that her life with her Wesley and their three children Bonny, Darcy and April Lynn was a really good life, lots of love in it, that's what counts in a real good marriage.

THE END